Preparing Preschoolers

Preparing Preschoolers

An Easy-to-Use Nursery School Program with Lesson Plans & Teaching Aids for Parents & Professionals

Suzan W. Allen and Karen H. Talbot
Illustrated by Cindy Decker

International Standard Book Number
0-88290-160-5

Library of Congress Catalog Card Number
80-83029

Horizon Publishers Catalog and Order Number
4027

Fourth Printing, May 1987

Printed and Distributed in the
United States of America
by

**Horizon
Publishers &
Distributors**

—————

P.O. Box 490
50 South 500 West
Bountiful, Utah 84010

Contents

A Child's Plea To His Parents

Give me more than food to nourish me. Give me the warmth and the security of your love.

Let me enjoy all five senses. Give me plenty of things to look at, to feel, to smell, to listen to, to taste. And even some things to break.

Teach me to take my turn. Watch me play so you can see how I am trying to work out my problems and what I am up against.

When you tell me to do something, please tell me why I should do it. Let me feel that I am a contributing member of the family. And be sure to include me in making the family plans when you can.

Please don't keep me your baby when I want to feel grown up. Don't transfer your fears to me. I have enough of my own to cope with and I don't need any more.

Help me not to act when I am angry. But don't make me so afraid of showing anger that I lose my capacity to feel strongly about anything.

Let me learn bit by bit to bear pain, to want things but to be strong enough to postpone gratification of certain feelings I am not yet ready to experience.

Let me try out my new powers as my body develops—to creep, to stand, to walk, climb, jump and run when I am ready. Don't limit the natural needs of my body because you have some unresolved hang-ups.

Give me a little corner in the house that is all mine and nobody else's. I need moments of peace and quiet that cannot be invaded by anyone.

Give me my share of consideration and attention. I must know every day, even if for just a few moments, that I am the only one you are thinking about and loving.

Let me ask any question that pops into my head. Don't make me ashamed for having asked it, even if it seems stupid. And give me as honest an answer as you can. If you don't know the answer, please say so. It's good training to hear someone say, "I don't know, but I will try to find out for you."

Be patient with me when I don't do things very well at first. Remember I have so many things to learn and almost everything takes some practice.

Let me bear the consequences for whatever I do. I need to be punished as well as rewarded. And when you punish me, make sure the punishment fits the "crime."

Above all, grant me, without reservation, your debt to me—unconditional love. For if I know it is there, I will be able to give the same to my children—and they will be able to give it to their children.

Your Child

Author Unknown

Ways To Use This Book

The education of preschool age children in our society has become extremely important to parents, teachers, and other concerned adults. *Preparing Preschoolers* is designed for those preparing for, or in the process of teaching preschool children—parents, grandparents, teachers, aides, babysitters, church leaders, and others.

Preparing Preschoolers is a ready-to-use preschool course. It contains 14 units of study that are of particular interest to the preschooler. Each lesson within the units has specific objectives and a lesson plan that is easy to follow and written so a child can understand the concepts. The lessons are filled with interesting facts, creative learning activities, suggested arts and crafts, and exciting children's recipes. A separate unit is devoted to a child's physical educational needs with suggested exercises and games. Most any adult could, with limited preparation time, teach one of the lessons to a child.

Although the course is designed primarily for children four years of age, many of the activities could be done with a younger or older child. *Preparing Preschoolers* is the instructor's book of units. *Projects for Preschoolers* is the child's workbook that is filled with fun activities, art projects and teaching aids that coincide with the units in *Preparing Preschoolers.* They are to be used together but can be purchased separately.

Preparing Preschoolers is extremely versatile and can be used in many teaching situations such as in the child's home, preschools, day care centers, nursery schools, church nurseries, and neighborhood and school cooperative preschool efforts.

Teaching At Home

Preparing Preschoolers is ideal for a mother of preschoolers to use in her home. A mother knows her child's capabilities, attention span, and interests better than anyone and can choose those lessons that would help the child the most and be the most enjoyable to him. A child loves mother to be his teacher at this age, and he will look forward to his personal school time when he has mother's devoted attention. You'll find, as a mother, that it is fun to teach your child and watch as his learning becomes a joyful experience for both of you. Through this learning together, you will reap many personal rewards and have a good feeling that you have made a meaningful contribution to your child's day.

Dad and other older family members can also get into the act by taking turns teaching the little ones. You'll find that Dad or an older brother or sister will be much more eager to help with the teaching if you can hand them a lesson ready to use such as the ones in the book. Your child will soon find this learning business is fun, because he is receiving encouragement and appreciation from the people he loves the most.

We have also found that a mature babysitter can do an acceptable job of teaching a lesson when left with adequate instructions and materials. At least you can rest assured that your children are engaged in a meaningful activity when you are away instead of being glued to the television set.

Neighborhood Cooperative Preschool

Mothers with preschool-age children living in the same neighborhood have found it advantageous to form their own non-profit preschool. Someone in the neighborhood could take the lead on this and invite several mothers over to talk about forming a neighborhood cooperative preschool. Each mother that agreed to participate would be responsible for teaching her share of days. This, of course, would depend on how many mothers and children were involved. Two mothers may want to team teach for a period of time and then alternate with the next pair of mothers. The units and lessons in *Preparing Preschoolers* could be assigned out weeks in advance, and if a mother that was assigned to teach became ill, the lesson could be easily given to another mother. Then on her day, she could trade with the mother that was sick, and everyone would put in equal teaching time.

The use of the lessons in *Preparing Preschoolers* helps eliminate the concern of some mothers that another mother might merely babysit when it is her turn to teach instead of preparing a lesson. If each mother has a copy of the book, she can review and reinforce what the child has learned that day. If for some reason her child was unable to attend one day, a mother could give the lesson on her own to her child. This way, he would not get behind the others.

Chances are that every mother interested in participating in a neighborhood preschool will not have an adequate room to hold the preschool in her home when it is her turn. This problem can be taken care of in several ways. There may be a mother in the co-op that would gladly open her home on those days in addition to the days she teaches. If team teaching is involved, you might be wise to pair up a mother who has adequate room with a mother who doesn't, and let them work out any compensating particulars. Often times there may be a room in a church, school, or public building that you could use for little or no cost.

In a neighborhood co-op situation, it usually works out best for each mother to buy her own child's more expensive materials such as crayons, scissors, paints, and paste. These items could be easily carried by the child each school day in his own bag with his name on it. The less expensive items needed for the activities of the day should be donated by the mother teaching that day. Each mother will get her turn, and it seems to come out even. If there is a particularly special craft or treat planned that day that is rather costly to make, each mother could send some money or any other materials needed with the child in his bag.

As long as every mother understands her responsibility and commitment, a neighborhood co-op can run very smoothly and be a satisfying experience for both mothers and children.

School and Mother Cooperative Preschool

Many school districts are offering preschool programs at a minimal cost where the mother helps with the teaching. Formats vary, but usually each mother is expected to prepare one facet of preschool per week. This might be an activity, treat, story, or lesson. The school usually supplies the materials for crafts and activities, but again this varies. *Preparing Preschoolers* would fit in beautifully with this type of a program, as each day could be organized by assigning mothers to be responsible for part of the lesson plan. This would take a lot of pressure off many mothers that feel a bit hesitant to come up with activities and ideas on their own and would appreciate the extra help this book would give them.

Church Nursery Programs

Along with any religious instruction that the children might receive, most church nursery programs allow plenty of time for other activities such as arts and crafts, music, and group play. This book is overflowing with ideas and projects to make this part of the nursery time fun, exciting, and memorable. The children will learn to look forward to church day and the time they spend in their own class. A church nursery leader's biggest headache is finding last-minute substitutes that can be prepared in a short time. The lessons provided in *Preparing Preschoolers* help ease a lot of this pressure and give confidence to spur-of-the-moment volunteers.

Preschools, Day Care Centers, and Nursery Schools for Profit

This teaching program provides at least nine months of lesson material, based on the assumption that a preschool is meeting between six and nine hours per week. It is an ideal program to use in a preschool situation for profit. Each child can have his own activity book all compiled and ready to use. This alone will save an instructor hours and hours of preparation time. The activities and art projects are creative, practical, and fun to do.

We have placed the units in a suggested order of study. However, you may want to vary that order according to the interests of your children and the time of year. The lessons in the holiday unit, for example, would best be taught a week or two prior to the particular holiday. A good time to teach the children about seasons is when they can actually see the changes outside if you live in a climate where this is possible. The ideas in the physical education and music units should be used in each lesson as they are needed.

How To Organize and Operate A Successful Preschool For Profit

Organizing and operating a preschool of your own can be very profitable and enjoyable, especially if you have a preschooler yourself that can participate in it. Preschools, day care centers, and nursery schools all vary according to the number of children, location of the school, and the amount of time a child spends at the school. It is our intention to give you some guidelines and suggestions of how to organize and operate a preschool that meets no longer than nine hours per week and enrolls no more than 25 children.

Most states have specific laws and regulations you must comply with before you begin to operate a preschool, which may vary from state to state. Therefore, we will not attempt to give you specific laws or requirements, but simply make you aware of what might be expected if you decide to open a preschool. We have also included suggestions regarding personnel, physical preparations of the school, advertising, registration, parent and child orientation, insurance, policies and rules, teaching resources, schedules, calendars, record keeping, and other valuable information.

Licensing

Before you can legally operate a preschool for profit in your home or away from home, you must obtain a business license. You would need to contact your local city officials for the information regarding this license. If you are in a residential zone and wish to hold the preschool in your home, directives concerning this license come under what is called the Home Occupation Ordinance for your particular city. It is generally a very inexpensive license, but you must comply with certain regulations before a license will be issued to you.

Generally you will be required to have a form signed by any neighbors within 300 feet of your house in each direction stating that they would not object to your holding a preschool in your home. That is approximately two houses on each side of you. At least two-thirds of the residents must give their approval.

After you have applied for your license, you can expect to have three visitors make inspections of your intended preschool facility, one each from the fire department, city inspection department, and the County Board of Health.

The fire department will look for such things as proper construction, safe exits, acceptable floor and wall coverings, smoke detectors, fire extinguishers, and any obvious fire hazards. If you plan to hold a preschool in your basement, there must be an exit to the outside from the basement level. Again, each fire department may have different requirements, so you would need to call and ask your local fire chief.

The city inspection department will probably look to see that the room is finished and has proper exiting. They will also look for hazards to small children such as wobbly steps, lack of hand rails where needed, loose nails, or cracking paint. Both the fire department and city inspector will check to see that you have the proper amount of square footage per child in the classroom area. You will probably be safe with 35 square feet per child. This is exclusive of a separate kitchen area, hallways, closets, or any unusable floor space. Some cities require more stringent regulations if ten or more students will be attending the school, such as an additional exit, more fire equipment, and off-street parking.

The County Health Department will check to see that the room(s) is clean and sanitary. Any toys used by the children are to be cleanable; tables and chairs must also be washable. Restroom facilities must be adequate and sanitary. There must be a toilet for every 12 children. A clean towel is required for each child, so the best way to provide this is to have paper towels for their use. Good lighting is essential in the classroom, and the Health Dept. will probably check to see that it is adequate.

Business licenses must be renewed each year, preferable thirty days before they expire. Operating a preschool as a business venture without a license is a misdemeanor punishable by law.

Director and Other Personnel

The director of a preschool should be at least 18 years old and be a high school graduate. Any special training in child care and education would certainly be a plus. The home could not be a better training ground, so if you are a mother of preschool children, you are probably very qualified to undertake such an adventure. An organized director with love and patience for children will be successful.

Many preschool directors have found that it is advantageous to have a partner or co-director with whom to work. In other words, you would have a team teaching situation and share responsibilities as to lesson preparations, etc. A word of caution—If you are contemplating this type of an arrangement, make sure you sit down before you begin and write up an agreement regarding what to do with profits, spending procedures, what you will buy, and where you will hold the school. You may be friends and neighbors, but while you are still friends, this is the time to sit down and negotiate. This may eliminate any problems later on that you cannot anticipate at this time.

A general rule to follow is that you need one staff member for every 10-15 children of preschool age (three and four year olds). Any more than that, and you would need an additional staff member. As long as one of you is at least 18 years old, this extra staff member could be 16 or 17 and act as an aide. At no time should a group of preschoolers be larger than 25 children. Before you begin registering students, you will want to check with your city zoning department for the regulations concerning the number of students you can have in a residential preschool.

Physical Preparations and Equipment

A preschool should have a minimum of seven areas, some of which can be the same floor space but used for different activities at different times. They are (1) classroom, (2) snack area, (3) kitchen, (4) play area, (5) learning center, (6) coat and bag area, and (7) restroom.

Classroom

The area where instruction, art projects, stories, etc., take place is the classroom. It should be large enough to allow 35 square feet per child. This would be exclusive of hallways, closets, etc. This room should be furnished with enough tables and chairs to comfortably accommodate the number of children in the preschool. The chairs and tables should be child-sized, so that they can work and sit comfortably. A hollow wooden door that has been painted with several coats of varnish makes a teriffic child's table. Detachable legs can be purchased at any hardware store to go on the door. Oftentimes school districts have old furniture sales and you can pick up good equipment for a reasonable price. This classroom area could also be used as the snack area.

Snack Area

A mid-morning or mid-afternoon snack should be served to the children each day. It is a time that children really look forward to. A designated spot needs to be identified as to where the snacks will be served and eaten. This is for the director's benefit more than the child's. If the children are permitted to wander during snack time, you can imagine the mess you would have by the time they were all finished. (The snack area could also be the classroom tables where they could sit down.) If you are fortunate enough to have nice weather, a porch or yard outside would be a nice place to serve a snack.

Kitchen

It would be ideal to have a kitchenette built right off the preschool, but if you are holding preschool in your home, your own kitchen should be more than adequate. Children delight in helping prepare and serve snacks and treats. Most of the food experiences in *Preparing Preschoolers* involve the children. A bar or table they can sit around to watch and help would be nice. Just a reminder—all children should wash their hands with soap and water before being allowed to handle or eat the food.

Play Area (inside and outside)

The children need to have a place to play when they first arrive at school and during breaks. If inside, the toys should be safe, durable, and washable. Shelves and boxes should be provided so that toys can be put away easily and neatly by the children. Often a corner of the classroom would accommodate such a need.

When the weather is nice, outside play is always fun for the children. The yard should be fenced and of adequate size to accommodate the number of children playing. Where the children are not playing for extended periods of time, a minimum of playground equipment is necessary. A swing set, monkey bars, tire swing, teeter-totter, sand pile, and play house are just a few suggestions of play equipment that could easily be set up in the backyard of an average suburban home.

Learning Center

No two children ever seem to finish an art project or worksheet at the same time. To prevent those that finish first from disturbing those that are not, a place must be designated as to where the child can go while waiting for the children. This area could be called the Learning Center and could be a corner of the classroom. A child can go here to look at books or engage in a quiet activity. If you make it too fun, the other children will want to quit working and join them. No toys should be allowed at this time, or the others will certainly want to investigate and leave what they are doing prematurely.)

Coat and Bag Area

A closet, hallway, porch, or small room should be equipped with a two-pronged coat hook for each child that he/she can reach. A rectangular bag 9″ x 12″ with a drawstring at the top should be made for each child out of denim or another strong fabric. The child's name should be written on it. You could ask the mothers to make their own child's bag or you could make them and add the cost onto the registration fee. Some mothers are slower than others about getting the bags made, so you may want to have them there for them to pick up the first day. The child needs to be taught to bring the bag to school with him each day. In it he will bring any show and tell items or special materials. He will take his own bag home each day with his art projects and special crafts stored safely inside to be shown off when he arrives. Any special instructions or notices for parents could also be sent home in this bag. Each child should be assigned an individual hook to hang his coat and bag on. If overboots are worn, they should be placed directly underneath the hook until needed again.

Restroom Facilities

The restroom should be easily accessible to the children. In other words, they shouldn't have to go up two floors and wander through the house in order to find it. There would need to be at least one toilet for every twelve children. The restroom should be clean and sanitary with plenty of soap, warm water, and clean towels. There must be individual towels for each child, so the best way to fill this need is to use paper towels that can be thrown away after they are used.

Supplies

Buying and gathering supplies for a preschool is a major part of getting started. If the supplies are put in certain boxes and containers and organized well, they will last longer, be easier to find when you need them, and will be less apt to get lost. For example, you will need to buy each child a small box of crayons and write his name on the box. The teacher should pass out the crayons to each child, and when they are finished gather the crayons up and put them all in a box labeled crayons. The same should be done with paint brushes, scissors, paste and paints. Plastic containers with lids are especially good for storing paper clips, brackets, and other small items.

Before investing a lot of money in major equipment such as cassette recorders, film projectors, or copying equipment, check at your local libraries and resource centers. Most of this type of equipment is available for the public to check out at no cost or a minimal fee. You will probably want to invest in a record player, as most facilities do not check these out for public use.

Individual chalk boards can be made economically by cutting plywood into pieces approximately 9″ x 12″ and then spraying one or both sides with special chalk board paint available at most hardware stores.

You will be using a great deal of paper in a preschool, so it is much more economical to buy it by the ream. Sometimes your paper distributors (listed in yellow pages) have self service centers where you can buy paper cheaper than retail or school supply stores. It might be well worth a phone call or two to check on prices before purchasing.

Listed below are the basic supplies you will need for the activities and arts and crafts suggested in this book:

SUPPLIES

poster paints	paper cups	drinking straws
envelopes	paper hole punch	paper sacks (several sizes)
masking tape	scissors	butcher paper
stapler	pencils	popsicle sticks
scotch tape	construction paper (all colors)	glitter
elmer's glue	paper clips	heavy paper
paper	brackets	black board
crayons	scraps of cloth	flannel board
string	pelon	
paper plates	yarn	

Advertising for Students

Usually a phone call to your neighbors announcing that you are going to offer a preschool will start the ball rolling, and you may have enough children sign up from mothers passing the word around. Another excellent way of advertising is to take an attractive, informative flyer around to the houses in your neighborhood. Include on the flyer:

1. Your name and address and any impressive credentials you might have
2. Your phone number and hours to call
3. Age of children invited to attend
4. Days of week and hours it will be held
5. Monthly charge (optional, you could tell when they call)
6. Registration date
7. Dates preschool starts and ends

If you operate a good preschool, you will find that "word of mouth" will be your best form of advertising. This, of course, will only benefit you after you have operated for a few months.

Insurance

Before you start operating a preschool, whether at home or at another facility, you need to take out some insurance for your protection and those children that are in your care. You would need to consult an insurance agent for professional advice as to the coverage you would need. He will probably suggest that you get comprehensive general liability, particularly if you are holding preschool in your home. This will cover the children for any bodily harm that may come to them and any property damage that may occur at the preschool or on a field trip in the name of the preschool. Chances are you may never have a serious accident, but it only takes once to make you very grateful you had insurance. Shop around, as rates vary according to the company and the amount of coverage. It is well worth the amount you will pay and quite inexpensive, particularly if extra coverage can just be added to your homeowner's policy. Insurance can legally be declared invalid if you are not properly licensed to operate a preschool.

Registration and Monthly Fee

You will have to determine what you are going to charge per month for each child. Your price should be based on the number of hours you will be holding preschool per week, the kinds of activities you will be doing and the overhead that you expect to have. Calling around to other preschools and finding out the going rate will help you come up with a reasonable figure.

When people call and express an interest in enrolling their son or daughter, you need to give them a date when they can register their child. At that time, you will want to collect both a registration fee and the last month's school fee. A registration fee does several things for you:

1. It helps you get set up with supplies, etc., until you start seeing a profit.
2. It makes parents more committed after they have enrolled their child, and you will have less drop-ins and drop-outs.
3. It can also be used as a deposit that can partly be refunded at the end of the school year if the child is always picked up on time or if the monthly charge is paid on time.

A registration fee should not be too steep, or it will discourage parents. A guideline might be that the fee is no more than the cost of two weeks of preschool. A registration fee should not be refunded if the child quits during the school year, as a general rule. You can use your discretion on this, particularly if the child has a prolonged illness or accident.

By the end of the first week of instruction of a new month, monthly payments should be paid by the parents. We would suggest that you do not give refunds for a student missing days that he has paid for. Not only would your bookkeeping get chaotic, but you'll have students miss more than necessary if there is no financial commitment involved.

It is advisable that you collect the last month's fee at the time of registration also. This, too, tends to commit parents and protects you from families who may take off on vacations, etc., and forget to pay that last month. It also discourages parents from dropping their child out in the middle of the year after you have made plans and financial commitments for that child.

At the time the child signs up, a registration form needs to be filled out with the following information:

1. The child's full name, birth date, current address, and date of enrollment.
2. Current name, home and employment address and telephone numbers of parent(s).
3. Current telephone numbers or instructions as to how the parent(s) may be reached during the hours the child is at preschool.
4. Current names, addresses and telephone numbers of person(s) authorized to take the child from preschool.
5. Current names, addresses, and telephone numbers of person(s) who can assume responsibility for the child in the event of an emergency if parent(s) cannot be reached immediately.
6. Name, address and phone number of child's physician and dentist.
7. Health information including medical report, chronic physical problems, vaccination and immunization history, and pertinent social information on the child and immediate family.
8. Written authorization from parent(s) for emergency medical care.

Parent Orientation

An hour or so needs to be set aside before preschool starts for a parent orientation meeting. This could be combined with registration day. At this time, you will want to go over such things as curriculum, school policies, payment procedures, and the school schedule. This meeting also gives you a chance to talk to the parents about their child and any special needs he/she might have. At this meeting, you need to supply the parents with a written sheet that includes the following information:

1. Philosophy and objectives of your preschool.
2. Name, address, and telephone numbers of both the director(s) and the place where the school will be held.
3. Hours and days preschool will be held; yearly schedule stating any holidays and vacation times.
4. Procedures for the handling of illnesses and emergencies of children.
5. Procedure for transportation of children on field trips.
6. Explanation of registration and monthly fees; payment procedures.
7. Information concerning programs, show and tell, snacks, insurance, and required materials.

Preview Home Visit

After a child has registered, it would be a good idea to go to the child's home and introduce yourself to him. Take with you a colorful party invitation to give to him, inviting him to the first day of school. Tell him to be sure to bring his mother along the first day so she can see his school and meet the other children. Just having met you tends to relieve a lot of fears and anxiety a child might have concerning a school situation, and he will look forward to his first day with you.

First Day of Preschool

Mothers are invited to come to preschool the first day with their children. An hour is usually long enough to keep them this first time. After introductions and a welcome to everyone, you will want to engage both mothers and children in an activity. A suggestion would be to have each child lay down on a piece of butcher paper and have his mother trace his outline. Then they can together fill in the face, hair, and clothes. The next day you could have each child's picture that they made mounted on the walls around the room and have each child find his own picture.

Another suggestion would be to make fancy name tags to tape above their coat hook. These could be made of construction paper and decorated with glitter, buttons, ribbons, etc. When finished each child could tape his name above his hook so he will know right where to put his coat and bag the next school day.

Cupcakes or cookies with children's names written on some and "Mom" written on others could be served with punch as a special snack, after which the mothers and children could be dismissed until next school day.

Rules

You will want to create an atmosphere that is relaxed and comfortable for the children. This is probably their first school experience, and it is important that it be a positive one. You also want to teach the children courtesy and responsibility, so rules need to be established and followed. Below are a few suggested rules for the children to learn.

1. Raise hand when wanting to talk or answer a question. Only one person is to talk at a time.
2. When teacher is talking, no one else should talk.
3. Each child is responsible for hanging up his/her coat and bag.
4. No hitting each other.
5. No throwing of toys, paint brushes, papers, or any other objects.
6. No more toy play after they have been put away for the day.
7. Everyone is expected to help clean up after each activity. (You may want to give out special helper badges as an extra incentive.)
8. Everyone lines up before going out to play and each child must have his coat on if it is cold.
9. Each child must stay in the snack area until he/she has finished eating. (No child should be forced to eat if he prefers not to.)
10. No child should come to school if he/she is sick. (This would also include a runny nose, new rash, or slight fever.)

You may want to set other rules, especially where the child's safety is involved. This would, of course, be determined according to your individual circumstances.

Suggested Daily Schedule

Preschools vary, but generally they meet two or three times per week for two or three hours each time. The following is a suggested daily schedule that you might want to use. The hours could be adjusted to your personal preference regarding starting and stopping times.

Daily Schedule

8:30- 9:00	Preschool personnel arrive and set up
9:00- 9:15	Children arrive and have free play with the toys and socialize with one another
9:15-10:00	First half of lesson and activities planned for the day
10:00-10:30	Recess: to include P.E., singing, dancing; a chance to wiggle and unwind
10:30-11:00	Snack and clean up; show and tell time
11:00-11:40	Second half of lesson and activities
11:40-11:50	Get ready to go home; put papers in bags and get coats on
11:50-12:00	Children are picked up to go home
12:00-12:30	Preschool personnel clean up

Monthly Calendars

We would suggest that you send a monthly calendar home with each child to give to his parents. Put on it the units or any special activities the child will be doing each day. This way the parents can ask questions about what the child has learned when he comes home. They can also reinforce concepts that have been taught.

If the child is to bring a shoe box or some other thing on a certain day, it can be put on the calendar with a star by it for extra emphasis. It is also nice to put any of the children's birthday dates on the calendar.

A good rule to follow regarding holidays and days off is to go by the same school schedule of the school district you are in. If the older children have a day off, so do the younger ones in your preschool. It also seems easier for parents to remember when the child has a day off if the holiday coincides with nearby schools.

Financial Records

Whether you are in business for yourself or with someone else, you are required to file state and federal income tax forms regarding the operations of your business. Therefore, you will need to keep accurate records of all your financial doings involving the preschool. Whether you show a gain or a loss, you must file.

If you are holding a preschool in your home, you would be wise to consult a tax adviser regarding special compensations and deductions for the use of your home as a business.

Businesses are required to apply for a federal tax identification number. Information regarding this is available at your nearest Internal Revenue Service office.

Keep all of your receipts for any expenses you may incur for supplies, equipment, mileage for field trips, salaries, etc. Buy a receipt book and record every check or cash payment that you receive from the child's parents. You will also want to keep a ledger of all of your outgoing checks or cash.

Keeping accurate records will also help you make financial projections for another year.

Show and Tell Time

Show and tell time gives each child a chance to be in the spotlight and share something with the other children that is special to him/her. It could be a toy, insect, picture, letter, or any number of things that might be important to that child at that moment.

There should be a special box for show and tell items. As soon as the child arrives, he should put his show and tell item in the box until his turn comes to show it off. After show and tell, the item should be put back in the box until time to go home. It should not be a play thing that day. Each child can bring a show and tell item once a week on the day his teacher assigns him. This should be consistant so that the parents will always know which day of the week is his so they can remind him.

Additional Teaching Resources

The quality of teaching can always be improved by bringing in outside teaching resources. People in the community are usually courteous and very willing to come and talk about their occupation or talent. This is always fascinating to a preschooler, as he is curious about these people. The following is a list of possible guests you may want to invite to visit your preschool:

forest ranger	military person	mother with new baby
policeman	beautician	store manager
fireman	barber	telephone operator
nurse	veterinarian	school teacher
doctor	farmer	taxi driver
dentist	banker	bus driver
druggist	musicians	secretary
plumber	athletes	pilot

It is also interesting for children to have different ethnic groups come in to talk about their heritage and share a special native dish. A handicapped person that is blind, deaf, or in a wheel chair can be asked to come and explain how he compensates for his handicap and tell how he would like others to communicate and treat him.

Movies and Visual Aids

Most libraries have short movies that can be rented very inexpensively that are educational and entertaining for preschoolers. A list of titles and subjects is available at your library. Slide and movie projectors can usually be checked out of the library, and you could use a white wall or sheet as a screen to show them.

Field Trips

Children love to visit new and interesting places in their community. Many places are appropriate for a preschooler to visit, and many are not. You would need to use your discretion and ask yourself, "Will there be plenty of interesting things to see, or will a child get bored after a few minutes?" Always call ahead and make appointments at the places you want to visit, and be sure to give the size of your group and the ages of the children. Some places do not allow preschoolers to come and visit, such as a police station; but they will gladly send a policeman to your preschool to talk to the children.

An idea for keeping children together on field trips is to give each adult a rope and have the children she is in charge of hold on to the rope in a line. Children seem to like this better than holding on to each other's hands.

Travel is getting so expensive, that if a guest can come to you, it may be just as effective and cost a lot less.

The following is a list of some suggested places to visit that usually welcome preschoolers:

fire station	railroad station	county fair
zoo	shopping mall	orchards
dairy	museum	cannery
farm	fish hatchery	bakery
grocery store	bird aviary	library
fast food chains	park	elementary school
airport	greenhouse	child's theatre

Transportation

Parents of the children could take turns providing transportation and acting as additional chaperones on field trips. When you do transport children in a vehicle, you may want to follow these suggestions:

1. Require written permission from parent(s) for transportation of a child to and from the excursion in your vehicle or in vehicles volunteered for transportation use, such as another parent's car. This written permission should be obtained at the time of registration.
2. Do not permit a child to remain unattended in a vehicle at any time.
3. Children should remain seated while the vehicle is in motion with seat belts buckled whenever possible.
4. Children should be loaded and unloaded at the curb on the side of the street where your destination is located.
5. Doors should be locked at all times while the vehicle is moving.
6. Any vehicle used for transportation of children shoud be enclosed.
7. Preschool age children should not be in transport longer than 30 minutes each way.

Unit I
Myself and Others

The Child's Name
Lesson 1

Objectives

At the end of the lesson each child will be able to:

1. recognize the initials of his first and last name
2. tell what a nick name is

Discussion

There is no one just exactly like you in the whole world. You are a very special person. Soon after you were born, your parents decided on a name that was especially chosen just for you. Everyone has a first and last name. What is your last name? Usually every person in your family has the same last name as you do. One set of your grandparents will probably have the same last name as your Dad and you.

Some people have more than just a first and a last name. They have what is called a middle name, because it comes in the middle of your first and last name. (Give some examples of middle names such as Betty Sue Smith, Tyler James Jones, etc.) Do you have a middle name? Some people like to be called by their middle name instead of their first name. Other people go by a "nick name." This is a shortened version of their first or middle name. For example, Susan can be called Suzy or Sue; Rebecca can be called Becky; Richard can be called Rich or Rick; and Robert can be called Bob or Bobby. A nick name can also be some affectionate name that your family or friends made up for you. Do you have a nickname? Oscar on Sesame Street has a nickname—Grouch! I hope you don't have that for a nickname!

The first letters of the words in your name are called your initials. Sometimes people are even called by their initials for a nickname. For instance, Tyler James could be called T.J. for short. What are your initials?

Activities

1. **1-1-1*** Make a name badge as shown. Write the child's name for him on the badge. Pin the badge on the child's shirt or blouse or punch a hole in the top of the apple and put a string through the hole and tie it around the child's neck to make a necklace.
2. Let the child draw a picture of himself with crayons or paints on a plain piece of paper. Write his name on it and the date. Send it home with him to keep in a scrapbook.
3. Let the child help you make his initials out of Initial Cookie Dough using the recipe in the recipe section. Frost and eat.

or

4. Make pancakes and form each child's first and last initials with the batter. Cook and let the child eat them.

Note on Visual Aid Numbering System

*Throughout this book, visual aids will carry a three-number code. The first number refers to the unit, the second number refers to the lesson, and the third number indicates the activity. The activity book, *Projects for Pre-Schoolers,* contains all the visual aids, and presents them in the same numerical order as they are introduced in this book. See its table of contents for assistance in locating the visual aids.

Our Body
Lesson 2

Objectives

At the end of the lesson each child will be able to:

1. identify and name at least five body parts
2. tell what a shadow is

Discussion

There is no one that looks exactly like you. Even identical twins, if you look closely, do not look exactly the same. If someone drew a picture of you, what would he put on it? (hair, eyes, ears, mouth, arms, legs, hands).

What color is your hair? What color are your eyes? Even our skin has a color to it. We can sometimes tell what race a person is by his skin and hair color. We all look different in many ways.

Have you ever gone outside and seen your shadow? A shadow is made when the sun shines on the front of you so it can't shine on the ground behind you. If someone else is with you, how do you tell your shadows apart? Our shadow looks and moves like us. Watch your shadow—it will do what you do. If we stand in certain places, our shadow goes long and skinny or short and fat. Shadows are fun. They make two of you, at least for a few minutes. Trees, houses, bikes, and mountains all have shadows at certain times of the day when the sun is shining down.

Activities

1. **1-2-1** Instruct the child to work on the concept of same and different by making the twins look the same.
2. **1-2-2** Instruct the child to put the person together in the proper manner.
3. Make a hand puppet—you will need:

felt   pen
scissors   glue or needle and thread

Pin two felt squares together. Lay the child's hand on top with the thumb and little finger spread apart. Trace his hand, leaving one inch from the hand all the way around. Cut along the pen line; glue together. Decorate as desired with face, hair, etc.

 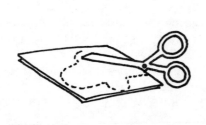  

4. Make a silhouette picture. Darken a room and have a child sit sideways in a chair against a white wall. Turn a lamp so it shines on the child and casts a shadow. Trace the child's silhouette onto a piece of paper.
5. Make gingerbread people and let the child decorate one to look like himself. Use frosting and candy.
6. Instruct the child to lay down on a big sheet of butcher paper, at least the length of the child. Trace around him and let him fill in the eyes, mouth, nose, clothes, etc.

My Emotions and Feelings
Lesson 3

Objective

At the end of the lesson each child will be able to name two emotions that a person can feel and demonstrate these emotions by using facial expressions.

Discussion

We all have different feelings called emotions. Some of the emotions we can feel are anger, fear, love, sorrow, and joy. Things happen to us during the day that change the way we feel. If someone is happy to see you and gives you a big hug, it will make you smile. If your older brother takes your toy away, you might feel angry and frown. When something happens that makes you all excited and stirred up inside, you react in an emotional way. What are some other things that make you excited and act emotional? (Santa Claus, Holidays, games, injuries, etc.)

Little babies also have emotions. Every baby cries when it is frightened by a loud noise or when something is making him uncomfortable. As the baby grows, he develops more emotions. If a baby touches a hot stove, he will experience the emotion of hurt and even anger. He will also learn to fear the stove or other hot things. A baby also learns from the people who take care of him. He learns love from his family and soon knows that a kiss on the cheek means you like him. He learns to smile by you smiling at him.

We can often tell what emotion a person is feeling by looking at his face or by the sound of his voice. When you have planned to play outside and it starts to rain, your face will probably look sad until the rain stops or you find something fun to do. If you do not obey your mother, her voice might sound angry until you mind her.

Many of the emotions we feel are pleasant, like joy, love, and excitement. Some are unpleasant, such as fear, anger, and sorrow. Anger is a strong emotion. No one can help getting angry at times, but we need to learn to control our anger. What are some of the ways we can show anger? (shouting, yelling, hitting). Some children throw themselves onto the floor and kick and scream when they get angry. This isn't the way we should act, is it? Starting now, you can learn to control your anger, and as you get older it will get easier for you.

Fear is an emotion that you have all felt at some time. You might be afraid of something because it scared you or hurt you at another time. Sometimes this helps you to be more careful. The baby who was burned on the stove is afraid, but that is good because she probably won't get near the stove again for a while. There is nothing wrong with being scared of cars when you cross a busy street. It makes you be more careful. We are often scared of things because we haven't tried them. If you have never been swimming, you may be afraid of the water. But if you take swimming lessons from an adult, you will soon know how to swim and won't be afraid of the water any more. What are some of the things you are afraid of?

Another emotion that we have all felt is sorrow. How do you act when you feel sad? Do you cry? Sometimes we cry when we are sad or angry. It's not fun to be sad; but when we feel happy again, it feels so good that it makes us never want to be sad again.

Emotions are really wonderful things, because they help us be the kind of person we are.

Activities

1. **1-3-1** Instruct the child to show a happy and sad face on the girl by moving the eyes and mouth.
2. Let each child take turns acting out different emotions on his face and actions such as crying, laughing, etc.
3. Read the story of Snow White. Go over the different emotions and moods of the seven dwarfs.
4. Sing the song, "If You Chance to Meet a Frown" found in the music unit. Let the children take turns turning the frowny face to a smiling face. A visual aid to the song is included, **#3-2-4.**
5. Help the child find different faces in magazines that express emotion. Together determine how that person is feeling.

Families
Lesson 4

Objectives

At the end of the lesson each child will be able to:

1. name the members of his own family
2. tell of two activities he enjoys doing with his family

Discussion

Each of you were born into a family so you could be taken care of. You needed someone to give you food, clothing, and a home. We live with our families because they care for us and love us very much.

Families can be all different sizes. How many people are in your family? A small family could be two people. A large family could have as many as ten members. Could ten people sit around your dinner table? Some families do not have children, but they are still a family. Some families do not have a father living with them, but they are families anyway. All families are different, but what makes them special is that they love each other. No matter what the size of your family, it is your very own, and that is what makes it important.

Activities

1. Make a family glove—you will need:

one glove per child	bits of felt
cotton balls	sequins
string	yarn

Stuff a cotton ball into each finger of a soft glove and tie it in place with a string. Sew on or glue sequins, glitter, and bits of felt for faces. Yarn can be attached to give each head a hairdo. The child may want to use each finger for a member of his family. If he does not have five, he can use a pet to fill in or imagine that he has more in his family.

Discussion (continued)

Families do lots of things together—play, work, sing, go on vacations. Families like to take trips together, especially to see other relatives like Grandma, Grandpa, and cousins. What was the last trip you took with your family? How did you get there? Did you walk, or go by plane, car, train, or bus? It doesn't matter how you got there or how long you stayed, as long as you were together as a family and had fun.

We celebrate special days with our family members such as birthdays, Christmas, Easter, and Thanksgiving. We work together as a family to take care of our home and other belongings. The members of your family are your best friends, because they love and care about you more than anyone in the whole world.

Activities (continued)

2. **1-4-2** Make a trip book—you will need:

old magazines	plain paper
scissors	stapler
glue	crayons
	pencils

Help the child make a trip book by cutting out pictures in magazines of things he would like to do with his family. Instruct the child to paste the pictures on pieces of plain paper. The child can draw pictures also to add to his book. Place the cover provided over the pages and staple the book together.

3. Make "Surprise Rolls" with the children to give to their families. Find the recipe in the recipe section.

Parents
Lesson 5

Objectives

At the end of the lesson each child will be able to:

1. name two things our parents do for us
2. name two things we can do to help our parents

Discussion

It is so fun to see our dads, especially when they get home from work. We know our dads love us and work very hard to give us a home and food to eat. Not everyone calls his dad, "Dad." Some children call their dad father, daddy, papa, or pop. What do you call your dad? Activities always seem more fun when Dad is around. Many dads like to take us camping, fishing, and hiking. Others like to read us stories and take us to ball games. It doesn't matter what we do with Dad, as long as we get to be with him. Our dads do a lot for us. What are some of the things you can do for your dad? (Run and get him something when he asks; help him in the yard; be quiet while he is resting or reading the paper; pick up our toys; put our bikes away before he gets home; save him the biggest piece of dessert).

We also love to be around our mom. Some children have different names for their mom such as mother, mommy, or ma. Moms also like to do fun things with us such as read books, take us to the store, make cookies, sing songs, and draw pictures. Moms do so many things for us. They wash our clothes, make our beds, fix our meals, and take care of us when we are sick. What are some things you can do for your mom to help her? (Don't fight with a brother or sister; empty the garbage; pick up toys; help set the table; tell her she is pretty.)

Activity

1. **1-5-1** Instruct the child to complete the worksheet on parents.

Discussion (continues)

Our mothers and fathers are older than us and know a lot about things that we don't understand yet. They know what is right and wrong and what is good or bad for us. Sometimes they ask us not to do certain things because they know it would be unsafe or harmful for us. When we do what our parents ask us to do, we are obeying or minding them. It makes our homes a lot happier if we obey our parents.

Activities (continued)

2. (Make a Dad)—you will need:

nylon stocking	felt
coat hanger	cotton scraps
yarn	buttons

Pull the wire coat hanger into an oval as shown below. Pull the nylon stocking over the coat hanger and tie it at the neck. To make a face, use cotton scraps, yarn, felt, and buttons. Tie a cotton scrap in a bow at the bottom for a bow tie. Let the children take turns role playing Mother and Dad with the puppet.

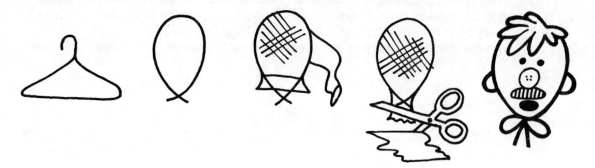

3. **1-5-3** Make the Mom and kids' stand-ups.

Other Family Members
Lesson 6

Objective

At the end of the lesson each child will be able to:

1. name two other members of families besides parents
2. name at least one thing he can do to make another family member happy.

Discussion

Some families have other members in them besides you and your parents. If there are boy or girl children, the boys are called your brothers and the girls are called your sisters. It's nice to have a brother or sister in your family. You always have someone to play with and someone to share your toys with. Have you ever noticed how hard it is sometimes for a little brother or sister to share? They have to learn that sharing is fun, because it makes the people we are playing with happy. If we have a brother or sister that has a toy we want to play with, we must ask before we take it and start to play. We might break or ruin something that is very special to one of our brothers or sisters, and that might make someone very sad.

Activities

1. Help the child make a treat to share with his family. A suggestion would be to buy the packaged bisquits. Cut them into fourths and deep fry them in grease until golden brown. Drain on a paper towel briefly and then roll them in sugar to make doughnut holes.
2. **1-6-2A, 1-6-2B** Help the child make the sack puppets of a brother and sister.

Discussion (continued)

There are still others in our family that we enjoy being with. Can you guess who they are? Our grandparents are members of our family, even though they may or may not be living with us in the same house. Grandparents are the parents of your father and your mother. Your father's parents have the same last name as you do. What is it? The other set of grandparents is your mother's parents. Their last name is different from yours. What is their last name?

If you live near your grandma and grandpa, you probably get to see them often. They love to see you. It makes them happy when you come to visit. If you live far away from them, you must write letters and send them pictures so they can see how you are growing. Sometimes you may get to talk to them on the telephone. We love our grandparents very much and need to show our love to them often.

Activities (continued)

3. Make a Popsicle picture frame—you will need:

glue	gold spray paint
macaroni	picture of child
popsicle sticks	

Paste the sticks together at the corners, spray the frame with gold paint, and put a picture of yourself in it to send to a grandparent. A polaroid snapshot would work great for this, or any grandparent would love a picture the child had drawn of himself.

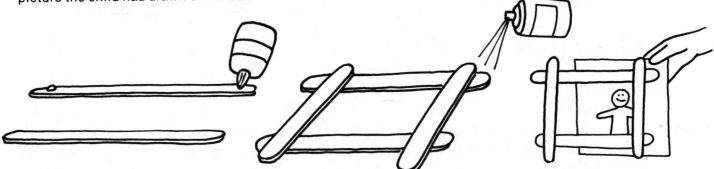

4. **1-6-4** Instruct the child to complete the worksheet on matching family members.

5. Invite a grandma and grandpa in your neighborhood to come and visit the class. You might ask them to come prepared to tell the things they like to do with their grandchildren.

6. Suggest that each child visit his own grandparents.

Babies
Lesson 7

Objectives

At the end of the lesson, each child will be able to:

1. name two ways babies need special attention and care,
2. name at least one way he can help mother with a new baby.

Discussion

Your family was so happy when you came to live with them. Most babies, like yourself, are born in hospitals. After about four days or so you were old enough to come home with your mother. Did you look like you do now when you were a baby? Of course not. How are you different? (Bigger, more hair, stronger, taller, teeth, can walk and talk.) When babies are tiny, they need lots of attention and care from their parents. They need their diapers changed many times a day and night. They also need to be fed, dressed, and bathed with the help of their parents or another adult. Babies can't do much of anything for themselves until they get a little older like you.

Babies can't use our beds, chairs, and tables yet. They need to have their own baby furniture that is just their size. They sleep in a crib, eat in a high chair, and sit in a special infant seat. All this special furniture helps keep the baby safe and happy. They even have special toys such as rattles and squeeze toys they can put in their mouths without choking.

Activities

1. Have the child bring with them today a washable dolly. Then let the child give his baby a bath, either in a small tub or you could use a wet wash cloth.

2. Make a doll cradle out of a shoe box using the directions and pictures on the next page to help you. You will need:

shoe box with top	scissors
pencil	brackets

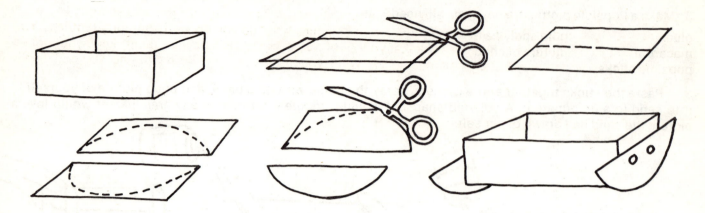

Discussion (continued)

Babies need to grow and learn lots of things. At first, the only thing they seem to do is sleep and eat. In a few months, they learn to do more things. Can you think of the things they might learn to do? (Sit up, crawl, talk, eat by themselves, etc.)

If you have a baby at home, you can help take care of it too. When it cries you can talk to it and play gently with it. You may want to give it a rattle or pacifier that it has dropped. You can be a big help to mother by getting diapers for her so she can change the baby, or being very quiet while the baby is asleep. What are some of the things you could do around the house that are quiet while the baby is sleeping? (Read, draw pictures, put together puzzles, etc.)

Activities (continued)

3. **1-7-3** Do the baby sequence worksheet.
4. **1-7-4** Let the child put together the baby with its different accessories.
5. Let the child make a creative picture using a baby bottle. Fill the bottle with poster paint and let the child drip the paint in a design of his choice on a piece of plain paper.
6. Let the child decorate a baby food jar with construction paper, glitter, sequins, and bits of felt. Use playdough to cover the lid; it will dry and stay on. The child can use the jar to put his own trinkets in or give it to his mother to use for the baby's safety pins.
7. Sing "Rock-a-bye Baby" using instructions in music unit.

Helping Our Families
Lesson 8

Objective

At the end of the lesson each child will be able to name three ways in which he can help around the house.

Discussion

When we help our families do the work around the house, it gets done a lot faster and is more fun. Our mothers and fathers like us to help them. You are getting to the age where you can take on duties or jobs around your home. When you were a baby, your parents had to feed and dress you. Now you can feed and dress yourself. You learned how to button and zip and buckle and tie your shoes. Sometimes we need help doing these things, but you are learning how a little better each day.

It is fun to pick the clothes you want to wear for the day. But sometimes our moms and dads want us to wear a certain outfit. Maybe you are going somewhere special and you need to dress up. Have you ever wanted to wear shorts and sandals in the winter, and your parents had you wear warmer clothing and shoes?

When you get undressed at night and put on your pajamas, what do you do with your dirty clothes? You probably have a dirty clothes hamper or basket at your house. It would really help your family keep your house clean if you put your dirty clothes in the proper place. When your mom folds the clean clothing, you could help her by putting the clothes away in the proper drawer.

Activities

1. **1-8-1** Help the child make the shoe, and then let him practice tying.
2. Help the child make his own dirty clothes bag by following the directions and diagrams below. You will need:

2/3 yard of denim fabric 36″ wide   tape measurer
red bias tape and red thread   scissors
needle or sewing machine

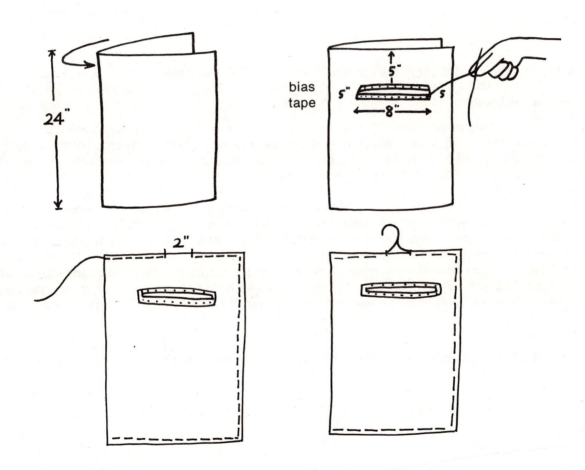

Discussion (continued)

A mother must work hard to prepare her family's meals. You can help your mother prepare some of the easier meals. You can also get things out of the fridge that your Mother needs and put them away when she is finished. You could even learn to set the table correctly. The fork goes on the left side of the plate and the knife and spoon go on the right side of the plate. The napkin is folded and put underneath or to the side of the fork. (demonstrate with a real fork, plate, napkin, knife and spoon)

Activities (continued)

3. Help the child make woven placemats that he can use at home. Fold a 8½″ x 11″ piece of paper in half. Starting at the open edge cut through the paper, leaving about one inch before the folded edge. Make cuts every one or two inches as shown below. Take another piece of paper and cut strips about two inches wide. Let the child weave the strips in and out of the first piece of cut paper.

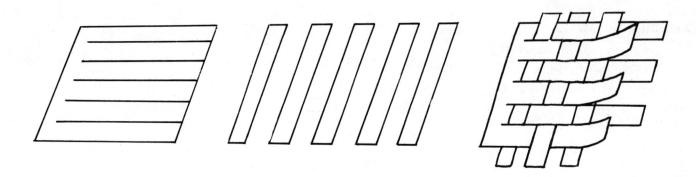

4. **1-8-4** Instruct the child to complete the worksheet on setting the table.

Discussion (continued)

We have lots of fun playing with our toys and games at home. Some of us have trucks, cars, blocks, trains, and balls. Others may have dolls, doll furniture, buggies, and music boxes. When all of these toys are spread out around the house, they can make a great big mess. Do you put your toys away when you and your friends are finished playing with them? If we don't put them away, what happens to our toys? (broken, lost) We can really help our mothers by learning to put our toys away when we are finished with them.

Our mothers and fathers spend a lot of time cleaning our house. They vacuum, sweep, wash dishes, dust, clean windows, scrub bathrooms, and make beds. They have so much to do that it's nice when we can be their helper. What are some things that you can do to help? (set the table, pick up toys, help make your bed, pick up clothes, dust the furniture, tend a little brother or sister briefly, etc.)

For those of us that have yards outside to take care of, there are lots of ways we can help outside also. You can pull weeds, water flowers, help plant a garden, and rake leaves. A lawn mower is very dangerous, so you must never try to mow the lawn or play near a lawn mower. It has very sharp blades on it and could cut you.

Activities (continued)

5. **1-8-5A, 1-8-5B** Find the job chart. Let the child paste the helping hands on the chart when he has completed the tasks.

Manners at Mealtime and at Play
Lesson 9

Objectives

At the end of the lesson each child will be able to:

1. name and demonstrate at least three proper table manners
2. name and demonstrate at least three courteous manners he should use while playing with other children

Discussion

Have you ever noticed that we need a specific key to start our car or get into our home? There are also special keys we can use to get along more pleasantly with others. These keys aren't like the keys you start the car with; instead, they are called good manners. Good manners means being kind and thoughtful of other people. Letting kindness guide our words and actions is what good manners is all about. Good manners are needed every day and in every place we go—at home, school, and play. What are some key words we can use that show good manners?

Please	May I?
Thank-you	How do you do?
I'm sorry	Just a moment, please
Excuse me	

Very often the people we like the best live in our home with us. We sometimes forget to be as polite and nice to them as we should, because they are around us so much. This means we need to work at being kind and pleasant to our families and friends.

When we get up in the morning there are certain things we need to do to get ready for the day, such as brushing our teeth, washing ourselves, and getting dressed. The next thing you probably do is eat breakfast. Did you know there are good manners that we should use at meal time also?

1. Take small bites of food and never have your mouth too full.
2. When you have food in your mouth, do not try to talk or drink.
3. Chew your food well, but with your lips closed.
4. When you want something passed to you, say please.
5. When someone helps or hands you something, say "thank you."
6. If you pass something to someone and they say thank you, you should reply, "you're welcome."
7. Always use a napkin to wipe your mouth.
8. Before you leave the table, ask if you can be excused.

Activities

1. **1-9-1** Find the manner keys. Cut out the keys that say please, thank you, I'm sorry, and excuse me. (The others will be used in the next lesson.) Let the child earn the keys by doing what they say.
2. Let the children help you prepare a simple meal such as soup, cheese and crackers, carrot sticks, milk, and fruit for desert. Instruct the children to set the table correctly. With you acting as hostess, let the children eat and practice their table manners.

Discussion (continued)

Playing with other children is lots of fun, but there are also good manners we should use with our friends. Can you think of something you can do that shows good manners while playing with your friends?

1. Take turns playing with certain toys or being first in games.
2. Don't whine, cry, or fight when things don't go your way.
3. Ask before you play with someone else's toy or bike.
4. Be careful when you play with someone else's toys that you don't break them.
5. Don't leave other children out or tell them they cannot play with you and your friends.
6. Talk kindly to others and never hit or push another child.

Activities (continued)

3. Let the children role play some situations for the rest of the class where they might have to use the above manners.
4. Play games and relay races where taking turns and courtesies can be practiced and stressed. Some suggestions are found in the music and P.E. unit.

Manners Shown to Adults and Telephone Manners Lesson 10

Objectives

At the end of the lesson each child will be able to:

1. name and demonstrate at least three manners we should use while around adults
2. name and demonstrate at least two manners we should use while using the telephone

Discussion

In our last lesson we talked about manners we should use while playing with our friends. Manners are also very important when we are around older people, who appreciate courteous children. Do you ever go visiting with your parents to another adult's home? Can you think of some ways you can be polite and use good manners around adults?

1. When you meet a friend of your parents or any adult you could politely say, "How do you do?"
2. When you go to someone else's house or business with an adult, you should sit quietly and not run through the house or jump on the furniture.
3. If the adult you are with is talking to someone else, don't interrupt him with a question until he has finished what he is saying.
4. If you are given a cookie or other refreshment, always say thank you.
5. If you are invited to play with the other children in the house, you should do so quietly as to not disturb the adults while they are visiting.
6. When you are through playing, help pick up the toys and put them away before you go home.

Activities

1. **1-9-1** Cut out the remainder of the manners keys not used in Lesson 9. Let the child demonstrate how he can use each of these.
2. Make the Manner Monster according to the diagrams below. Use construction paper and glue to put it together. The manner monster is each child's reminder to use good manners.

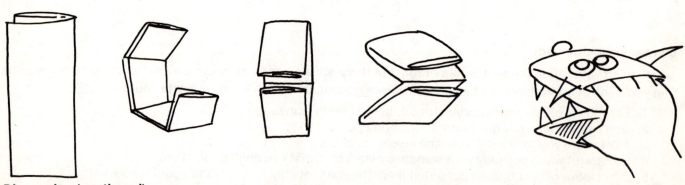

Discussion (continued)

You are getting to the age where you are able to talk on, dial, and answer the telephone. We all need to use good telephone manners. When you answer the phone, speak clearly and slowly so the caller can understand you. If the phone is for someone else, you should ask the person if he can wait a moment, please. Then go get the person the caller wants. Never yell the person's name into the phone; this could hurt the other person's ear. If the person the caller wants is not at home, you could offer to take a message or ask if he would like to talk to someone else. Always remember that the telephone is not a play toy. You should only use it to call those people you really need to talk to.

Activities (continued)

3. Help the child make a play telephone. Take two empty soup cans or paper cups and punch a hole in the bottom of each of them. Cut a string three to four yards long. Thread the string through each of the holes and secure the ends in each can. Make sure you thread the string from the inside of the can the first time and the backside of the second can. Let the child hold a can up to his ear while another child talks into his can. They can take turns talking to one another.

4. **1-10-4** Help each child put together his own telephone directory.

5. Help each child practice his own telephone number. Write it on his play phone so he can look at it and dial it.

6. Obtain some play telephones and let the children pretend to talk to each other or their parents or another caller. Have them practice the telephone manners you have talked about.

7. Bell Telephone has representatives that are very willing to come to some of the larger classes and talk about telephone manners and courtesies.

Unit II
Colors

Introduction to Colors and the Color Red
Lesson 1

Objectives

At the end of the lesson each child will be able to:

1. name three things inside and three things outside that are colored
2. name three things that are red

Discussion

Colors are all around us. Almost everything is colored . . . . a sunset, a field of flowers, a rainbow, fruit, Christmas tree lights, clothes you wear, your eyes and hair. Colors help us tell objects that are the same apart. If you have a ball and your friend has the same size ball, you can tell them apart if they are a different color.

Activities

1. Let the child look at himself in the mirror and determine what color his eyes and hair are.
2. Ask the child what his favorite color is, what his favorite ice cream color is, and what his favorite color of sucker is.
3. Make a colored collage. Gather colored items such as marshmallows, prepared cereals (Trix, Fruit Loops), bits of colored paper, colored toothpicks, etc. Let the child stick these items together with colored frostings. When he is finished he can eat the edible parts.

Discussion (continued)

There are two kinds of colors—primary and secondary. One of the primary colors is red. We see the color red on many things . . . . fire engines, tomatoes, apples, cherries, stop signs, strawberries, wagons, and traffic lights.

Activities

4. **2-1-4** Make a mobile of red things.
5. Make a red wagon. You will need:
   shoe box or match box   string
   construction paper   red paint
   brackets   scissors
Paint a small match or shoe box red to make a wagon. Cut wheels out of construction paper and attach them to the wagon with brackets. Hook a string in the front so the child can pull it along.
6. Blow up a red balloon and let the child play with it.

The Primary Colors Yellow and Blue
Lesson 2

Objectives

At the end of the lesson each child will be able to:

1. identify the colors yellow and blue and name one object that is blue and one that is yellow
2. name and identify all three primary colors in a review situation

Discussion

Yellow is a primary color. It is a bright, happy color that we find is the color of lemons, bananas, sunflowers, and the sun. The big yellow sun is a huge star that gives the earth light and heat. The sun is really a big firey ball.

Activities

1. Help the child make a sun out of construction paper or yellow felt. Cut a circle approximately two inches in diameter. Then take a straight piece of paper one inch wide and four inches long. Make small cuts through the width leaving a very small space at the end as to not cut all the way through. Curve the strip around the circle and glue both of them on a piece of paper. Then have the child draw something on the paper that the sun shines on.

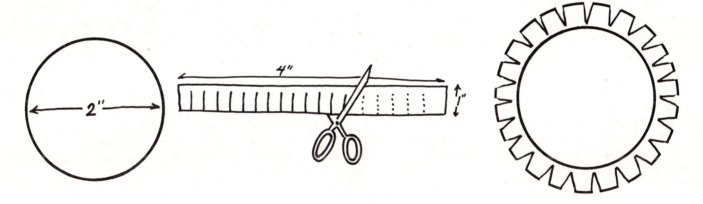

2. Make Frozen Bananas according to the recipe in the recipe section.
3. Make the "Lemon Cooler" found in the recipe section.
4. Write the child's name on a big yellow balloon with a washable magic marker or let the child make his own design. Spray the writing with hair spray and let it dry. Then blow the balloon up and let the child play with it.

Discussion (continued)

Blue is another primary color. It sometimes reminds us of cool things like oceans, lakes, rivers, and streams that are blue. Other blue things are the sky, bluebirds, and blue jeans.

Activities (continued)

5. Draw a simple sea and sky picture for the child. Instruct him to color the objects in the sea and sky with crayons. Then have him color over the picture with light blue water color. The objects will resist the water and show through the blue.
6. Blow up a blue balloon and let the child play with it.
7. 2-2-7 Make a spinner. Instruct the child to color each of the objects on the spinner with a primary color. Tape pieces of yellow, blue, and red paper around the floor. Let the child spin the spinner. Whatever color it points to, have the child go to the matching color taped on the floor and also identify it orally.

8. Cut squares of red, yellow, and blue paper. Put the colors in any order and instruct the child to tell you which is on top, in the middle, and on the bottom. Now change the order and keep quizing the child until he understands the colors and the top, middle, bottom concept.

9. Make 3-colored cookies found in the recipe section.

Secondary Colors
Lesson 3

Objective

At the end of the lesson each child will be able to:

1. mix two primary colors and tell what the new color is
2. name and identify the three secondary colors orange, green, and purple

Discussion

We can mix the primary colors red, yellow, and blue to get other colors. They are called secondary colors. When we mix red and yellow it will make *orange.* Blue and yellow mixed together will make *green.* Blue and red will make *purple.*

Activities

1. Take several jars of water and put food coloring in them. Make primary colors and mix them to get the secondary colors.

2. Make some playdough using one of the recipes in the recipe section. Divide it into three parts and color it with food coloring to make the primary colors. Now help the child mix them to make orange, green and purple.

3. Get some colored cellophane (red, yellow, blue). Place one color on top of the other to make the secondary colors.

Orange

What are some orange things? (pumpkin, orange, carrot)

4. Make an "Orange Julius" drink using the recipe in the recipe section.
5. Help the child carve a pumpkin.
6. Cut an orange in half. Dip the inside of the orange into orange tempra paint. Instruct the child to press the orange onto a piece of paper and repeat to make an interesting orange design.

Green

When we think of green, we usually think of spring when the green grass and leaves come out. Other green things are a grasshopper, celery, and green apple. Once a year we have a day when everyone is supposed to wear green or they get pinched. This is called St. Patrick's Day.

7. If the weather permits, go on a walk and find several new green things that are starting to grow . . . flowers, shrubs, trees, etc.

8. Make a green hat for the child to wear. You will need:

paper plate   stapler
scissors   green construction paper

Cut out the center of the paper plate. Let the child color the plate green. Cut two strips of green construction paper to criss-cross over the child's head to form a curve. Staple the strips across the hole in the paper plate to form an "X."

Purple

9. Instruct the child to dip his thumb in purple poster paint and press it on a white piece of paper. Repeat the process until the child has formed a cluster of grapes with the prints.

10. Teach children the nursery rhyme "Little Jack Horner". Let them play like they are Jack and hold up their purple thumbs as if it were the plum.

11. For a special treat, buy plum fruit leather at any grocery store or health store.

12. Have grape juice or toast with grape jelly.

Colors in Review
Lesson 4

Objective

At the end of the lesson each child will be able to name and identify the primary and secondary colors.

Discussion

Now that you have learned all the primary and secondary colors, lets see how well you can remember them.

Activities

1. **2-4-1** Make the clown spinner. Color each of the parts of the clown a primary and secondary color.

2. Play musical colors. Tape the six colors on the floor and put on some music. Have the child walk around the circle of colors. Stop the music periodically and have the child identify the color he is standing on.

3. **2-4-3** Find the color game sheet. Use the spinner to tell the child how many spaces he can move forward.

4. Play the fish pond game. Put six fish-shaped papers into a glass bowl, each the color of a primary or secondary color. Let the child fish for a colored fish and identify the color he pulls out.

5. Make a color cake. Mix any white cake according to directions and pour it into the baking pan. Next drop food coloring around the cake and swirl it with a knife. Bake the cake according to the directions.

6. Instruct the child to make a colored chalk drawing. Let him wet the ends of colored chalk and then draw on a white piece of paper.

7. Cut a circle four inches in diameter. Next draw lines through it to make six equal pie shaped pieces. Color each piece a different primary or secondary color. Take six clothes pins and color the ends of them a primary or secondary color to match the pie pieces. Instruct the child to clip the clothes pins around the circle at the section that matches the colored end of the pin.

8. Make a multicolored viewer. You will need:

popsicle sticks   colored cellophane
glue   egg carton
scissors   tape

    Cut windows in the bumps of an egg carton. Glue circles of colored cellophane over the windows. Tape on a popsicle stick for a holder. Let the child look through it and name the different colors.

Unit III
Homes

Homes of Long Ago
Lesson 1

Objective

At the end of the lesson each child will be able to name at least two types of homes used long ago.

Discussion

Our homes are the places we live in. It is believed that the very first kind of home used by man was a cave. This is a hole in the side of a hill. The caves were very dark inside because they didn't have any windows to let in light. The cave, however, protected people from the wind, rain, and snow. People that lived in caves were called cavemen.

The Indians who lived on the plains in America used tents for their homes. These tents were made out of animal skins. These Indians moved around a lot, so a tent or tepee was easy to move and put up again in a different place. These tepees looked very much like the tents we use to go camping in.

The early settlers in America built log cabins for their homes. They would chop down trees and cut off all the branches until they had a log. The logs looked much like telephone poles, and they were fit together to make walls. Logs that were split in half were used to make the roof of the log cabin, and stones from the land made a chimney for the big fireplace. Most log cabins did not have stoves like we do. Most of their cooking was done over an open fire. Today, up in the mountains, you can still see log cabins that were similar to the homes of the early settlers.

Activities

1. Help the children make a tepee out of blankets and chairs to play in that day. Or if you have a tent, that would be even better.
2. Go to a park and build a fire in one of the designated areas. Roast marshmallows with willow sticks. If you have a fireplace, that would work just great. Make Smores, a tasty treat using roasted marshmallows. The recipe is in the recipe section.
3. **3-1-3** Find the log cabin. Glue stick pretzels for logs onto the picture. Use toothpicks for logs, or you could roll cut brown paper on a pencil to form a log and glue them on the picture.
4. **3-1-4** Instruct the child to put together the tepee and Indians.

Homes People Live In Today
Lesson 2

Objective

At the end of the lesson each child will be able to name three types of homes people live in today.

Discussion

Today we find people living in a variety of different kinds and sizes of homes. What kind of home do you live in?

People who live on a farm live in a farm house. It can be a one-story house, with all the rooms on one floor; or it can be a two-story house with some of the rooms on the second floor. A farmhouse usually has a barn close by where all of the farm animals live.

Some people live in a big building called an apartment house. In apartment houses, there are many homes on each floor. People live on the top, bottom, and all the floors in between. Many apartment houses have an elevator that takes you to the floor you live on.

Many people live in what are called residential or suburb areas. Usually one family lives in each home. It has a yard in front and back where you can play.

A trailer house is another kind of home. It is a house on wheels. Usually the trailer can be hooked onto the back of a car or truck and moved from place to place.

Have you ever seen a houseboat floating on the shore of a river? This kind of home is used for vacationing or all year round. In China, lots of people live on small boats called "sampans." A great big boat that can sail on the ocean and all over the world is called a yacht. Many of the people who work on the yacht live on the boat all year round.

Activities

1. Find pictures of different homes, show them to the children, and let them guess what kind of home each is.
2. **3-2-2** Find the trailer house and truck. Hook them together.
3. Let each child try drawing his own house with crayons or paints.

Materials Homes Are Made Of
Lesson 3

Objectives

At the end of the lesson each child will be able to:

1. name three materials homes are made out of
2. recite his own address

Discussion

Do you remember the story of the Three Little Pigs and the Big Bad Wolf? They all made their homes out of different materials—straw, sticks, and bricks. (read story to children) What material is your house made out of?

If we walk up and down our street, we will usually find that each house looks a little bit different on the out-side. Some homes are made of bricks, some of wood, some of rocks. In alaska where it is very cold in the winter, many Eskimo hunters build a home out of snow. These are called igloos and are built of big blocks of snow. In some hot, dry lands people build their homes out of adobe. This is clay and straw mixed together that is formed into bricks and baked in the sun.

Sometimes houses can look a lot alike, but there is always one way we can tell our house apart from any other. It has its very own house number or address. Just as we all have a different name, all houses have a certain number that helps people find where we live. It also helps the mailman know where to deliver any letters that are for us.

Activities

1. **3-3-1** Find the Three Little Pigs' house, and let the child paste bricks on it.
2. Go for a walk and discuss with the child the different materials you see that houses are made of.
3. **3-3-3** Let the child make a neighborhood of houses. Cut out the fronts of houses. Paste them on jello or pudding boxes and place them around to make a neighborhood. Put the child's address on one of the houses and help him practice it till he can say it correctly.
4. Make an adobe house out of clay. Use a clay recipe in the recipe section and just add brown food coloring.

The Building and Design of a Home
Lesson 4

Objectives

At the end of the lesson each child will be able to:

1. name two workmen that help build our homes
2. name at least three rooms generally found in a home and what they are used for

Discussion

Our homes were built by many workmen. If your home has a basement, a man with a big shovel came to dig a hole for the basement. Another man came with a cement truck and poured cement to form the foundation for your home. Other men nailed boards in place with hammers, and a brick mason may have laid bricks on the outside of your home. A plumber put in the pipes to bring water into your home. An electrician put in wires for the lights, and a furnace man put in a furnace so you could have heat. A painter painted the house inside and out.

Before all of these workmen started, they had a plan to go by. They were told where and how many rooms to make. Our homes are built with different rooms to meet our needs and daily activities. What are some of the rooms in your house? Every home needs a *kitchen* where we can prepare and eat our food. We also store food and dishes in the cupboards or in the refrigerator. We need a *bathroom* to wash ourselves, brush our teeth, and use the toilet. Our *bedrooms* give us a place to sleep and put our personal belongings. A *living room*, or family room, is a place where we can relax and visit with members of our family or visitors that come to our home.

Activities

1. Make a sugar cookie house using the recipe in the recipe section and paint it with egg yolk paint, also found in the recipe section.
2. Get a stump or scrap of wood, a small hammer, and a large nail. Let each child carefully try hammering a nail into the stump. When several nails are in the stump, let the children stretch elastic bands back and forth around the nails.
3. **3-4-3** Help the child put the house together and the furniture inside.

4. **3-4-4** Go on a treasure hunt. Locate the different parts of the home pictured.
5. Make a house out of an 8½″ × 11″ sheet of paper following the diagrams below.

6. Make cookie "Stained Glass Windows." The recipe is found in the recipe section.

Safety in the Home
Lesson 5

Objective

At the end of the lesson each child will be able to name three things in the home that could be unsafe for a child and tell why.

Discussion

Many accidents can happen in homes as well as away from our homes. Our parents try to make our homes safe for us, but we must learn to avoid things that could be unsafe for us.

Have you ever hurt yourself by falling? Falling is a common home accident. Where are some places that you could fall in a home if you are not careful? (stairs, table tops, slippery floors, etc.) We need to be especially careful when using stairs. Always hold on to the hand rail and never run—always walk. Put your toys and skates where they belong, not on the stairs. They could cause a person to slip and fall. If you spill a drink, always wipe it up. You might fall on it later. If your mother has just mopped the floor, you must stay off of it until it dries, or you could have a bad fall. If you can't reach something, you shouldn't climb on the table or cabinets. Chances are you could lose your footing and tumble to the ground.

We must be very careful with tools, knives, or any sharp objects. If you need to use a knife or some scissors, ask an adult to find you some safe ones. Make sure you never run with anything that is sharp. If you are carrying something sharp, hold the sharp edge down away from you as you walk.

Of course, we all know not to play with matches or any kind of fire, don't we? What could happen if we played with matches? We could burn ourselves or start a terrible fire and burn our house down! (review fire safety rules found in fireman lesson) Plugs or electrical cords should never be played with. We could get a bad shock or a burn. What are some other places in our homes that can burn us? (stove, iron, furnace) Never climb up on or get too near a stove. You never know when it might be turned on or where you might accidentally turn it on and get burned. Irons are also very hot. We shouldn't play by the iron while someone is ironing.

In our homes we have special cabinets where we keep medicines. Medicines help us when we are sick, don't they? They are not candy! We should only take medicines when our parents give them to us. If we take the wrong medicine, or too much, it can make us very sick. Some medicines can even be poisonous, if they are not meant for us or if we take too much of them. Have you ever seen "Officer Ugh?" He has his hands over his mouth that tells us not to put certain things into our mouths. You might see him on certain medicines and many cleaning bottles.

We should never put beads, money, buttons, or little toys in our mouths. If we swallowed them, we could choke. Food, drinks, and our toothbrushes are the only things that belong in our mouths. Small objects do not belong in our nose or ears either. Never put anything in your ears!

Many times your mother will store vegetables, fruits, and breads in plastic bags. We should never use these plastic bags for play toys. They can be very dangerous if we put them on our heads, because we would not be able to breath and would soon die. A refrigerator that is stored in someone's basement, garage, or yard should never be used as a toy. Don't close a child in one or ever hide in one yourself. Once a person is inside, he cannot get out without someone's help. There is not enough air to breathe inside, and we must breathe in order to stay alive.

Never let a stranger into your home. A stranger is someone you do not know. Even if the stranger says he knows you or your parents, run and get an adult before you let him in. If you cannot see who is at the door, don't answer it. Wait for an adult to help you.

Activities

1. **3-5-1** Help the child do the worksheet of safe and unsafe things.
2. **3-5-2** Make an "Officer Ugh" puppet.
3. Make an extention cord holder to keep plugs safely put away. Let the child cover an empty toilet paper roll container with material or contact paper. Fold the cord and put it inside.
4. Demonstrate to each child what he should do if he finds a plastic bag around the house. He should tie it in knots and never play with it. (tie a bag in knots)
5. Let the children practice falling slowly down to the ground for a P. E. activity.

Unit IV
Shapes

Circles
Lesson 1

Objectives

At the end of the lesson each child will be able to:

1. recognize and properly draw a circle
2. name two objects that are round like a circle

Discussion

We call things that are round in shape circles. Circles seem to be everywhere you look. The plate you ate your breakfast on this morning was probably round like a circle; or if you had cereal, your bowl was in the shape of a circle. The buttons on your clothes that you put on this morning are probably circles. Can you think of some other objects that are round and in the shape of a circle? (Show the child round objects such as a plate, sucker, wheel, doughnut, ball, balloon)

Activities

1. **4-1-1** Find the Birthday Party picture. Discuss the picture with the child and find the different things that are in the shape of a circle. Have the child trace the round objects first with his finger, and next with a pencil.
2. Instruct the child to practice making circles on a small black board or piece of paper. To properly draw a circle have the child start at two o' clock and go around counter clockwise.
3. Now that the child knows the proper way to make circles, have him go back to the Birthday Party picture and trace around the circle objects with a crayon or pencil.
4. Help the child find circle objects around the house that he can put on top of a piece of paper and trace. Find bigger ones and small ones. Some examples might be a cup, plate, bowl, button, dime, cookie cutter, bottle cap, soup can.
5. Make the blow bubbles using the recipe in the recipe section. Let the child blow the bubbles to form different sized circles.
6. Make a circle clown. The supplies you will need for this activity are:

small paper lunch sack	popsicle stick
cotton ball	colored paper
string	yarn
newspaper	glue or paste
scissors	salad plate
buttons	

Make a clown by tracing around a salad plate on a colored piece of paper to make a head. Paste on buttons for his eyes and nose and paste a piece of yarn on for his mouth. Cut a triangular-shaped hat to fit on the head and paste a cotton ball at the tip of the hat as shown on the next page in the diagram. Open the lunch sack and stuff it with crinkled newspaper, leaving two inches at the top. Tie the top of the lunch sack with some string and spread the excess at the top of the sack to form a collar for the clown. Take strips of colored construction paper for arms and legs and fold them in an accordian fashion. Glue them to the sack in the proper positions. Paste the clown's head to the popsicle stick. Then put a small amount of glue on the bottom of the stick and push it into the top of the paper sack. If the child wishes, yarn could be added to the clown's head for hair.

7. Make a necklace by cutting a piece of yarn and stringing cereal on it. The supplies you will need for this activity are:

Cherrios (or any round cereal with a hole in the middle)
yarn
scissors

8. Make a circle flower. Draw a circle on a piece of construction paper. Cut into the circle and roll the ends with a pencil. Paste on a paper and add a stem and leaves.

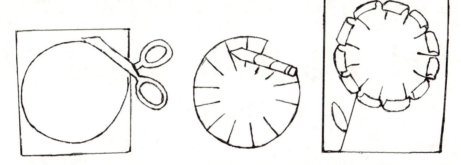

9. Make cupcakes for a special treat today using a cake mix or one of the recipes in the recipe section.

Triangles
Lesson 2

Objective

At the end of the lesson each child will be able to properly identify and recognize a triangle.

Discussion

Another shape that we are going to learn about is the triangle. Triangles are a little harder to find than the circles that we discussed in the last lesson. Triangles have three corners and three sides. (Show the child a triangle) Can you count the sides and corners? Ships sails are often in the shape of a triangle. Many trees take on the shape of a triangle. The roof of your house might be in the shape of a triangle.

Activities

1. **4-2-1** Find the Playground Picture. Help the child find the things that are in the shape of a triangle. Have him trace the objects first with his finger and then with a pencil.

2. Have prepared ahead of time several triangles in different sizes. Also mix in a few circles with them. Show the child the different shapes and have him identify them. After he has identified them correctly, instruct him to trace the shapes on a piece of paper and then cut them out.

3. Make a triangle crown for the child. Cut a strip of paper the size of the child's head, leaving two inches extra to fasten in a circle. Cut out triangles and paste them onto the strip of paper all the way around. Staple the crown to fit the child's head.

4. Cut out two triangles and paste them together to make a star.

5. Make a triangle hat for each child out of newspaper as shown below.

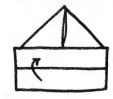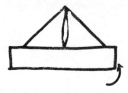

6. **4-2-6** Instruct the child to do the worksheet on triangles.

7. Make a triangle flower. Cut a piece of colored paper in the shape of a triangle. Cut one end. Roll the ends with a pencil. Make a stem and paste it on.

8. Have sandwiches for lunch today. Cut the child's sandwich into two triangles.

Squares and Rectangles
Lesson 3

Objectives

At the end of the lesson each child will be able to:

1. properly identify and recognize the shape of a square and rectangle.
2. name one object that is square and one that is rectangular.

Discussion

The square is another shape. It has four sides that are all the same length and it has four corners. (show the child a square) Can you count the sides and corners? Many objects are square such as blocks, some windows and pictures, and a piece of bread.

Activities

1. Cut some squares for the child. Instruct him to trace the squares on a blackboard or piece of paper.
2. **4-3-2** Find the Playroom picture. Discuss the objects that are square and have the child trace them first with his finger and then with a pencil or crayon.
3. **4-3-3** Let the child build the Dog House using squares.

Discussion (continued)

The last shape we are going to learn about is a rectangle. Like the square, it also has four sides and four corners. However, all of its sides are not the same length. The top and bottom are the same length and the two sides are the same length, but the sides are either shorter or longer than the top and bottom. Let's look at a rectangle and see just what this means. (Show child a rectangle)

There are lots of things that are rectangular in shape. Most of the books you look at are in the shape of a rectangle. Your front door is a rectangle and so is the pillow you sleep on.

Activities

4. Arrange some rectangles and squares on a table. Have the child pick out what you ask for—a square or a rectangle. Have him tell you why it is a square or a rectangle. Keep doing this for a few minutes until he understands the difference.

5. Find some boxes or plastic food containers with lids that are square or rectangular in shape. Instruct the child to match the lids with the correct box and tell you whether it is a square or rectangle.

6. **4-3-6** Find the worksheet on squares and rectangles. Instruct the child to complete it.

7. Have sandwiches for lunch and cut the child's sandwich in half to make two rectangles. Then cut one of the halves in half to make two squares.

8. For a special treat, make the Graham Cracker Goodies using square and rectangular-shaped graham crackers. You will find the recipe in the recipe section.

Shapes in Review
Lesson 4

Objective

At the end of the lesson each child will be able to properly identify and recognize a square, rectangle, circle, and triangle.

Discussion

Now that we have learned all of our shapes, let's review them to make sure we remember what they all are.

    a. Circle—round
    b. Triangle—three sides, three corners
    c. Square—four equal sides, four corners
    d. Rectangle—top and bottom equal; two sides equal; four corners

Activities

1. **4-4-1** Find the figure ground worksheet. Instruct the child to match the shapes.

2. Make sugar cookies using the recipe in the recipe section. Cut the cookies into the four different shapes that you have studied and then bake and frost them.

3. Play Musical Shapes. Cut out several of the four different shapes and tape them in a circle around the floor. Stop the music at different intervals and call out the name of a shape. The child should then stand on the shape you have named.

4. Go for a walk. Give each child a small sack with the shapes of a circle, square, rectangle, and triangle inside to take with him. Tell the child to find something that is the shape of each of his papers. When he has found all four shapes, he can return and look for four more on his way back.

5. Cut out several of the four different shapes. Instruct the child to color the shapes and then paste them on a paper to form funny looking creatures as shown.

6. Help the child make a paper cup out of a square of wax paper or plain paper:

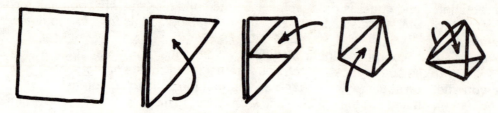

Start with square, fold in triangle, fold corner over the fold, other corner in, fold top down on both sides. Fill with water and let the child drink.

Unit V
Senses

Sight
Lesson 1

Objectives

At the end of the lesson each child will be able to:

1. name three activities for which we need our eyes
2. tell how light affects the pupils in our eyes

Discussion

Our eyes are very important. They help us see what we are doing and where we are going. The sense of sight aids us in our daily activities such as walking, eating, and playing. Eyes come in different colors. What color are your eyes?

Activities

1. Instruct each child to *close his eyes* and walk a short distance to a designated spot in the room. (Most children will only go two or three steps before opening their eyes.)
2. Blindfold the child and give him a paper and crayon. Instruct him to try to draw a picture.
3. Play "Eye Spy". Describe something in the room and let another person try to guess what it is. (take turns)

Discussion (continued)

The little black dot in the center of the eye is called the pupil. It lets light into your eyes. If it is bright, the pupil gets smaller. If it gets dark, the pupil gets bigger to let in more light. Sometimes on a very sunny day the sunlight is so strong it hurts our eyes. We wear dark sunglasses to protect them.

Some people can see better than others. Many people with eye problems wear glasses to help them see better and strengthen their eyes. A person who is always in the darkness and cannot see at all is called blind. Many blind people have what is called a "seeing eye dog." This dog is trained to guide the blind person. He can help a person cross the street, go to school, or find his way home. Blind people read by using special books made of braille. Braille is raised dots that stand for different letters. He runs his fingertips over the dots to read.

Our eyes are very fragile and we need to take care of them. We should never poke things in our eyes or rub them. Our hands are germy, and we will put dirt into our eyes. We have tears to help wash out our eyes. Our eyelashes help catch lint and dust and keep it from getting into our eyes. When our eyes are tired we should lay down and shut them so they can rest.

Activities (continued)

4. Go into the bathroom with the light on and have the child look at his pupils. Turn the light off for a while and stay in the dark bathroom. Then turn on the light and have the child look at his pupils. They will be much larger.
5. **5-1-5** Make a pair of glasses for the child.
6. Instruct the child to look briefly through a magnifying glass or someone else's glasses.
7. Blindfold the child and have him feel a couple of objects and guess what they are. Examples: toy, apple, book.
8. Instruct the child to color a piece of paper with crayons using any colors except black. Now have him color over the picture with a black crayon very heavily. Give the child a bobby pin and let him scratch the black crayon off the picture to reveal the colors underneath in a design of his choice.

Smell
Lesson 2

Objectives

At the end of the lesson each child will be able to:

1. tell which feature on our face we use for smelling
2. name two other functions of the nose

Discussion

Your nose tells you when something smells good or when something smells bad. Like your ears, your nose can work in the dark. You can tell what is cooking just by the smell it gives off. You can also tell when a skunk has been around or if a campfire is burning.

Activities

1. Prepare ahead of time cups of different ingredients that give off a strong scent. (Examples: cinnamon, perfume, peanut butter, vinegar, pine needles) Cover the tops of the cups with foil and punch small holes through the foil. Instruct the child to smell each cup and try to guess what is inside.
2. Instruct the child to go on a hunt and find two good smells and two bad smells. Then have Mom or teacher guess what they are.
3. Bake homemade bread or cookies for a special treat today. Let the child guess what kind they are by the aroma given off while baking.
4. Take the child for a walk outside and find four smells. (Examples: flowers, rain, pine tree, dirt)

Discussion (continued)

We also breathe through our nose. If we have a cold and our nose is stuffed up, we have a hard time breathing and smelling things. Our nose also helps us taste things better. Cookies always taste better when we can smell them.

Activities (continued)

5. Take two or three sachet tablets and wrap them in netting. Tie with a ribbon. Let the child put the tablets in his drawer to make his clothes smell better. You could also soak a cotton ball in perfume and put it in a drawer.
6. Blindfold the child and plug his nose for a second or two. While doing this, give him a drink of milk, water, or soda pop. See if he can guess what he is drinking.
7. Take an orange and have the child stick cloves very close to each other into the orange. The cloves will protect the orange from spoiling, so the child can keep it for months. The orange with the cloves will give off a lovely aroma to any closet or drawer.
8. Make homemade handcream using the recipe in the recipe section. This is a nice gift idea for the child to give to parents, friends or grandparents.
9. **5-2-9** Instruct the child to do the worksheet concerning the concept of same and different.

Taste
Lesson 3

Objectives

At the end of the lesson each child will be able to:

1. name the four tastes we find in food
2. name three functions of the tongue

Discussion

We taste things with our tongues. The tongue has 3,000 taste buds, which are the tiny bumps we find on our tongue. (Have child look in the mirror at his tongue and taste buds.) In tasting food, we find that it can be bitter, sweet, sour, or salty. (discuss foods that fit into each taste category)

The tongue not only aids us in tasting, it also helps us eat. It forces the food against our teeth and helps us swallow our food. The tongue also helps us talk and say our words correctly.

Activities

1. Place several white powdery ingredients in similar looking containers. Some suggestions would be flour, sugar, alum, powdered milk, soda, and salt. Instruct the child to taste each one and try to identify what it is and which kind of taste it is—sour, sweet, salty, or bitter.
2. Show the child the different sugar forms sugar can come in. (brown, powdered, granulated, cubed, honey) Have the child taste each one of these sugars. Point out that even though these sugars taste very similar, they look and feel differently.
3. Make homemade cookies for today's treat using many of the powders and ingredients the child tasted. Use the suggested recipes in the recipe section.
4. Draw a simple outline on a piece of paper of a ball, house, or animal. Put some salt in two or three separate containers and add food coloring or a little tempra paint and stir. Instruct the child to spread glue over the picture. Let him sprinkle the colored salt on the glue and then shake off the excess to make a salt picture.
5. Make homemade lemonade. Have the child taste the lemon rind (bitter), the lemon fruit (sour), and the finished lemonade (sweet). Together these different tastes make a delicious drink. Recipe found in recipe section.
6. Instruct the child to hold onto his tongue with his fingers and try saying such words as snap, duck, teeth, and splash.

Hearing
Lesson 4

Objects

At the end of the lesson each child will be able to:

1. distinguish between a loud and a soft sound
2. name two ways to protect our hearing

Discussion

We can tell that something is happening around us without seeing or touching by using our ears. If we close our eyes and are very quiet, we can hear lots of different sounds. Some sounds are loud like thunder, a door that has been slammed shut, or a hungry baby that is crying. Some sounds are soft like a pin that has been dropped, a kitty walking across the floor, or trees gently blowing in the wind.

Our ears are fragile and they can easily be hurt. We must never put things in our ears such as a pencil, toothpick, hair pin, or anything sharp. You should never shout in a person's ear or hit anyone on the side of the head. This could hurt the eardrum that helps us hear. A radio or television set that is too loud can also harm our ears.

Activities

1. Make different noises where the child cannot see what you are doing. Then have the child guess what you are doing by the sound you made. Examples: crumple newspaper, whistle, turn on the water, wash dishes
2. Instruct the child to find sounds around the house and have his Mother or teacher guess what sounds they are.
3. Hide an alarm clock that has a fairly loud tick in various places around the room. Let the child listen for the "tick" and guess where the clock is.
4. Have the child talk in varying degrees of loud and soft or hit a pan with a spoon with different degrees of force.

Discussion (continued)

Some people have trouble hearing. They wear a hearing aid which fits in the ear and makes the sounds louder. This enables them to hear better. Some people cannot hear at all, not even with a hearing aid. These people are called "deaf." They use their other senses to help them understand what other people are saying. They use a sign language, which is done by making different shapes with their fingers and hands that stand for letters and words. This way they can talk to others. Deaf people can also learn to read lips. They will watch very closely what your lips are saying and can understand you without hearing the words.

Activities (continued)

5. Mouth some familiar words for the child. Have him guess what you are saying. Have him watch television with the sound off and try to guess what is being said.
6. Show and teach him some simple sign language that deaf people use. Below are a few examples.

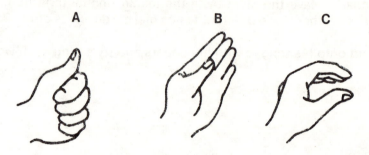

A   B   C

7. **5-4-7** Cut out the special listening ears for the child. When the child has them on, clap out different patterns of sounds and have the child repeat them just as you did it.

> Examples: clap, clap, clap
> snap, snap, snap
> stomp, stomp, stomp
> clap, clap, snap
> clap, snap, snap
> clap, snap, stomp

8. Make a horn by using an empty toilet roll. Secure wax paper over one end with a rubber band. Poke several holes in the wax paper with a pin. Instruct the child to blow thru the other end.
9. Make a drum by simply using an empty, round Quaker oats box. Put the lid on and you have a drum.

10. Make a shaker by taking two paper plates facing each other. Put rice or beans inside. Punch holes around the outside rim of the plates using a paper punch. Let the child lace the plates together with yarn. Color the plates with crayons or paints.

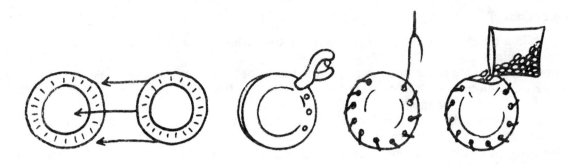

Touch
Lesson 5

Objectives

At the end of the lesson each child will be able to:

1. name one thing he can hold and touch hard and one thing he can touch softly
2. name three properties he can discover about an object solely by touching it

Discussion

The sense of touch is one way we feel love. When we like something, we want to touch it, hold it close, and cuddle it. You like to cuddle your stuffed animals, dolls, etc. Mom, Dad, Grandma, and Grandpa like to love and cuddle you.

We can hold and touch different objects either softly or hard. We must touch eggs, Christmas tree ornaments, kittens, and babies very softly or we could break or hurt them. But our balls, bikes, and many other toys we can touch and hold hard because we cannot hurt or break them.

We usually use our hands for touching. They can tell us many things about an object. We can tell whether it is hot, cold, round, rough, smooth, dry, wet, bumpy, hard, flat, or soft.

Activities

1. Get one of the child's most favorite toys and have him show how he touches and cuddles it. Then give the child a hug.
2. Blindfold the child and have him guess what the objects are in a bag by feeling them. Suggestions: ice cube, sandpaper, marshmallow, brush, rock, or sponge. Ask leading questions about its state such as, "Is it wet or slippery?"
3. Make finger jello using the recipe found in the recipe section. Let the child feel it and play with a small portion of it. Then give him a new plate of the jello to eat.
4. Make "oobleck" using the recipe found in the recipe section. Children love the feel of this and it is fun to play with. It washes off easily.

Discussion (continued)

We can also feel and touch with other parts of our body—toes, feet, lips, tummy, and mouth. We can feel when we are being tickled and we can feel in our mouths whether we are eating something crunchy, cold, or soft.

Another thing we feel is pain. It hurts us, but it is a good warning signal. If our shoes are too tight, the pain tells us to take them off so we don't get a blister. If we touch a hot oven, we feel the pain and take our hand away quickly. If we have an upset tummy, we can tell someone and get proper care.

Activities (continued)

5. Take the child around the house and have him feel the different textures. Let him feel the carpet, water in the tub, or even a plant.
6. Make finger paints using any of the recipes in the recipe section. Let the child make a picture of his choice.
7. Tap the child on the back with a pencil or finger. Have the child identify how many taps and then have him repeat the same pattern on the table.
8. Make a "texture" drawing. Place a piece of paper on top of some sand paper and color it. It would also work to use a flat heat vent or vegetable grater.
9. Wash and dry egg shells. Crumple them into fairly small pieces. Instruct the child to glue the egg shells onto a piece of paper and then paint them different colors.

Unit VI
Community Helpers

Introduction to Community Helpers and the Mailman
Lesson 1

Objectives

At the end of the lesson the child will be able to:

1. name four different community helpers
2. tell what the mailman does and name two ways mail is transported
3. tell what three things are needed on an envelope (stamp, receiver's address, sender's return address)

Discussion

There are all kinds of different people in the world. Some are tall, short, fat, thin, young, and old. Some have freckles, others wear glasses, some have blonde hair, and others have brown eyes. All of us look different, and all of us like to do different things. For example, some of us like to read books, while others would rather play dolls or jump rope. Grown-ups like to do different things too. People have jobs so they can earn money to pay for food, clothes, and housing. There are many different kinds of jobs that people have in the community where you live. (discuss different jobs) Examples: doctor, pilot, and fireman. (Discuss the jobs that the child's parents might have.)

Mailman

One community helper we can see almost every day is the mailman. What does a mailman do? A mailman drives a special mail truck or walks his route. He carries with him a big bag of mail. He delivers your mail and picks up any mail you have left for him to take to the Post Office.

Activities:

1. Have the child watch for the mailman that day and pick up the mail.
2. Help the child make his own stationery. Print around the edges of a blank piece of paper with poster paint or ink. Use one of the following methods:

a. Cut a small potato in half. Cut out a simple design from the center of one of the halves. Dip the cut-out half in paint and then press the potato on the paper.
b. Cut out a small figure from a sponge. Dip that figure in paint and press it on the borders of the paper.
c. Using an ink pad, press your thumb on the pad and then onto the paper. Draw stick legs, arms, and features to make figures.

3. Next have the child write a letter, with your help. Use the stationery the child has made. He may want to write a letter to Grandma, a brother or sister, or a teacher. Another suggestion would be to write a letter to himself. In this way, he can have the fun of watching for the letter to come back to him.

Discussion (continued)

In order for a letter to reach the right person, it needs to be addressed correctly. It must include the following things: (1) the person's name you are sending it to, (2) his street address, and (3) his city, state, and zip code. This information goes in the middle of the envelope. In the top left corner you put your return address. If for some reason your letter can't get to the person, the mailman sends it back to you. Last you put a stamp in the right-hand corner. This pays for all the work people must do to get your letter to the proper place. (Address the child's envelope for him.)

If your letter is coming into or going out of state, it will probably travel by airplane or truck. In the olden days, letters and packages were sent from place to place by "The Pony Express." There weren't any airplanes or trucks, or even mailmen. A messenger with a bag of mail would ride his horse as fast as he could until he reached a particular spot. Then he would stop and give the mail to another messenger who was on a fresh horse. Each place the Pony Express riders stopped was called a post. That is why we call our mail buildings post offices.

Activities

1. Play "Pony Express." Place the children in different spots around the room or in different rooms around the house. Let each child take his turn carrying a bag of mail, pretending he is riding a horse. The first rider should hand the bag off to the next child and stay at that post. The new rider now goes to the next child and hands him the bag of mail, etc.
2. Take the child to a post office and let him mail the letter he has written.

Doctors and Nurses
Lesson 2

Objectives

At the end of the lesson the child will be able to:

1. tell two reasons why we visit doctors and nurses
2. name at least two pieces of equipment a doctor uses and tell what their functions are

Discussion

One of the first people we come in contact with is a doctor. He helps bring us into the world when it is time for us to be born. Doctors have helpers called nurses. We visit doctors and nurses when we are sick and when we are well. They want to make sure we are growing properly. When we make a visit to a doctor, we are called a patient. Doctors and nurses both go to school for a long time to learn how to make people well. Your doctor is one of your very best friends, because he helps you stay healthy and strong.

Both doctors and nurses wear special clothing. The doctor usually wears a white smock-type coat. The nurse usually wears a white dress, white cap, and white shoes.

Activities

1. **6-2-1** Make the doctor and nurse finger puppets.
2. **6-2-2** Make a nurse's cap for the child.

Discussion (continued)

The doctor has special equipment he uses to check us. The following are just a few of the things he might use when he checks you.

1. *Tongue depressor*—a long, thin stick used to hold your tongue down while the doctor checks your throat.
2. *Special light*—about the size of a flashlight, but shaped narrow enough at the top so the doctor can check our ears and nose.

3. *Stethoscope*—the doctor puts the ends of this in his ears and places the round end section on your chest. He can hear your heart and make sure it is beating properly. (Have the child put his hand over his heart and feel it beating.)

4. *Hammer*—soft hammer made out of rubber used to check reflexes. (Hit the child gently with the side of your hand on his knee. The knee reflex should cause the leg to jump forward.)

5. *Thermometer*—a narrow glass tube used to take our temperature. This will tell the doctor or nurse if we have a fever. We sometimes hold it under our tongue.

The nurse usually weighs you and checks your height to make sure you are growing normally. She fills out a form on you for the doctor to look at.

Activities (continued)

3. **6-2-3** Fill out the physical facts worksheet about the child.
4. **6-2-4** Make a doctor bag from our pattern. Fill it with first-aid items such as Q-tips, Bandaids, vaseline, candy pills (Smarties), popsicle sticks, and packaged "Wet Ones."
5. Make tongue depressor people. Let child decorate a tongue depressor. Use markers to color the depressor, yarn or cotton ball for hair, and material or bandaids for clothes.

Police Officers
Lesson 3

Objectives

At the end of the lesson the child will be able to:

1. name at least four duties of a police officer and give one reason policemen are our friends.
2. cross the street safely by using the four basic safety rules.

Discussion

Men and women must go to school to learn how to become police officers. They learn to handle a gun, to be physically fit, and to keep cars and trucks moving safely on our streets. Policemen usually drive special cars or motorcycles. Sometimes they patrol streets by just walking up and down them. Policemen use special clothing to help us recognize them. If we get lost or in a car accident, a policeman will be glad to help us. He is our friend.

A policeman has special equipment that helps him perform his duties. He has a badge, gun, traffic whistle, radio, and handcuffs. Some of a police officer's duties are to:

1. help lost children get home safely
2. help people cross the street
3. help people who have car accidents
4. help people with directions on how to get places
5. stop people who drive too fast on the road or break driving rules
6. stop fights or people who are being cruel to others
7. help prevent damage to personal or public property

Did you know that no one in the whole world has the same fingerprints as you? When we touch things we leave our fingerprints on them. Have you ever touched a window and seen your fingerprints? Policemen often take fingerprints of people to identify them.

Activity

1. **6-3-1** Make a policeman puppet out of felt, colored pellon, or colored paper.
2. Help the child take his fingerprints. Press his fingers on an ink pad and then onto a paper. If an ink pad is not readily available, you could have the child rub his fingers across the black print of a newspaper. He will then have black fingertips that can be pressed on a white paper to make a print.
3. Take a big piece of butcher paper and let the child paint on it. Use one of our fingerpaint recipes.

Discussion (continued)

Policemen often help us cross the street safely, but they are not always around to help. We must learn how to cross by ourselves. Always follow these rules.

    a. Walk to a corner or a crosswalk, don't cross in the middle of the block.
    b. STOP before you begin to cross.
    c. LOOK both ways (left and right) to see if it is safe to cross.
    d. WALK across the street.

Activities (continued)

4. **6-3-4** Cut out pictures. Each picture represents one of the above rules. Have the child paste the pictures in order on a blank paper.
5. Take the child outside and practice crossing the street using the above rules.

Fireman
Lesson 4

Objectives

At the end of the lesson the child will be able to:

1. name two fire safety rules
2. demonstrate two ways to extinguish his clothes should they catch on fire
3. name two duties of a fireman and list two pieces of his equipment

Discussion

Men go to school to learn how to become a fireman. A fireman lives at the station 24 hours at a time (day and night). He must be ready, even at night, to jump in his fire truck and rush to a fire. He eats and sleeps at the station and keeps the fire fighting equipment clean and in perfect working condition.

The fire chief visits schools, factories, and stores to teach fire safety. He tells people to:

1. Never play with matches or electrical outlets.
2. Turn off irons, stoves, and other appliances when finished.
3. Put out all cigarettes and campfires when finished.

A fireman also tells us what to do if the clothes we are wearing catch on fire:

1. Remove the clothing as quickly as possible.
2. Throw water, soda pop, or anything close by you that is wet on the fire.
3. Drop to the ground immediately and roll until the fire is out.

Activity

1. Have each child practice the above rules so he will further understand them in case of an emergency.

Discussion (continued)

A fireman has other duties besides putting out fires. He can help us in almost any emergency. He can rescue your kitty if she gets caught in a tree, or help a little child whose arm is caught in a fence post. Firemen have also learned first-aid and can help in any medical emergency until the doctor comes.

A fireman has special equipment for fighting fires. He has a helmet, fire-proof coat and pants, ax, badge, gas mask, and walkie-talkies. His special boots go all the way to his knees. They have steel on the bottom of them so the fireman can walk on broken glass and not get cut. They have steel toes to protect his feet from falling objects. Once at the scene of the fire, the fireman works very quickly to get all of the people out of the burning building. Next he works to put out the fire.

There are two kinds of fire trucks. One is a pumper truck which is smaller and pumps the water. The other is the hook and ladder truck which is bigger and carries the equipment needed to fight the fire.

Every house should have a fire extinguisher in case of a fire. Do you have one at your house? Even boats and ships have fire equipment on them in case a fire starts at sea.

Activities (continued)

2. **6-4-2** Make each child a fireman's hat.
3. **6-4-3A, 6-4-3B** Find the fireman and his equipment. Cut out the equipment and paste it on the fireman in the appropriate places.
4. **6-4-4** Make a fire truck puzzle using the pattern provided.

Dentist and Teeth Care
Lesson 5

Objectives

At the end of the lesson the child will be able to:

1. name at least two functions of our teeth and explain that baby teeth are replaced by permanent teeth
2. brush his own teeth correctly
3. name two ways the dentist takes care of our teeth

Discussion

Our teeth are very important to us. They have three main functions or jobs: (1) to help us chew our food, (2) to aid us in our speaking, and (3) to enhance our appearance.

Everyone eventually has two sets of teeth. When we are small, we have what are called our "baby teeth." When we are between the ages of five and seven, our baby teeth fall out and our permanent teeth grow in their place. This is the last set of teeth we get, so we must take very good care of them.

Activities

1. Have the child put his lip over his teeth and try to talk. Give him an apple and tell him to try to take a bite of it without using his teeth.
2. Let the child look at his teeth in a hand mirror. Help him count them. He should have ten on top and ten on the bottom.

Discussion (continued)

When we eat food, especially food with sugar in it, it sticks to our teeth. If we don't brush this food away, it turns into dental plaque. This plaque eats away at our teeth and causes cavities. Cavities are little holes that eventually get bigger and bigger and ruin our teeth.

To keep our teeth white and free from cavities, we must brush them after every meal and visit our dentist every six months. Use a toothbrush with soft bristles. Brush your teeth the way they grow. The top teeth grow down, so brush them in a downward motion. The bottom teeth grow up, so brush them in an upward motion. Brush each spot in your mouth eight to ten times each. Always use a toothpaste that contains flouride. Brush your teeth for at least two minutes.

Activities (continued)

3. Help the child brush his teeth. Demonstrate the proper way as explained above.

4. Have the child paint a picture of his choosing using an old toothbrush for a paint brush. Dip the brush into poster paints and then brush onto the paper.

5. Make a dental floss picture. Fold an 8½"x11" paper in half. Dip a long strand of dental floss in the paint, leaving two inches hanging out of the end to hold on to. Lay the dental floss in the fold of the paper. Close the paper at the fold and press down with one hand. Now pull the dental floss through. Open the paper and you have a unique design. Lay it flat and let it dry.

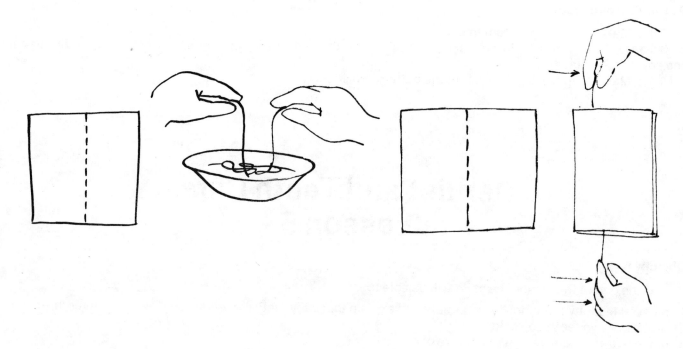

Discussion (continued)

A dentist is the person who helps care for our teeth. When we visit the dentist we find he has a special chair that goes up and down and turns around. You wear a big plastic bib that keeps your clothes clean. The dentist takes pictures of your teeth using an X-ray camera. He can find any cavities in your teeth by looking at the pictures.

The dentist scrapes the tarter or extra plaque off your teeth. He cleans them with a special toothpaste and special brush on his drill. He also polishes your teeth with a rubber buffer. If you have a cavity, the dentist fills it with silver or gold so the tooth will stop decaying.

Activity (continued)

6. Obtain some "disclosing wafers" from a drug store or your dentist. These are tablets that when chewed cover the bacterial plaque on the teeth red. Give each child a wafer to eat and then have him brush off the red. This way he can see where he missed brushing earlier in the lesson.

Unit VII
Numbers

Order of Numbers
Lesson 1

Objectives

At the end of the lesson each child will be able to:

1. recognize the numbers 1-10
2. put the numbers 1-10 in the proper order

Discussion

Numbers play an important part in our everyday lives. Mothers need them when they are cooking, sewing, or shopping. Dads need them when they are building, using the telephone, or paying the bills.

Activities

1. Go on a hunt and find things that have numbers on them. Talk about what each thing does and is used for. Examples: measuring tape, ruler, watch, clock, telephone, calendar, timer, thermometer.
2. Make a fun dessert for the child. Point out all the numbers on the package or recipe and tell what they call for. (explain that if you put too much or too little of an ingredient in the dessert it will not turn out as it should.)
3. Practice counting using your fingers. Sing "One Little, Two Little Indians" song.
4. Write the numbers 1-10 on a piece of paper and point to them. Have the child orally say them back to you. (Do not attempt, at this point, to have the child write the numbers.)
5. **7-1-5** Find the cash register. Instruct the child to cut out the numbers 1 - 10 and the cash register. Have the child paste the numbers in order on the cash register. Explain what a cash register does.
6. **7-1-6** Find the number train. Instruct the child to cut out all of the trains and then place them in the proper sequence according to the number on each train. (save the trains for the next lesson)
7. Tape the numbers 1-10 in a circle around the floor. Play some music on a record player and instruct the children to march around the numbers. Take the music off at different intervals and have the children freeze where they are. Each child should then tell you the name of the number he is standing on when asked.
8. **7-1-8** Instruct the child to do the dot-to-dot picture. Connect the numbers according to order.
9. Write the numbers 1 - 10 on small pieces of paper that are cut in the shape of a fish. Put all of the papers inside a big glass bowl. Let the children "fish" for a number. When he pulls it out, he is to identify the number he has caught.

Numbers and the Amount They Represent
Lesson 2

Objectives

At the end of the lesson each child will be able to:

1. point to the correct written numbers between one and ten when asked to do so
2. associate the correct number of objects with each of the numbers between one and ten

Discussion

A number represents a certain amount of objects.

Activities

1. Get out the trains that you made in the previous lesson. Staple a small envelope to the back of the train cars. Instruct the child to put into the envelope the proper amount of objects according to the number written on the car. Almost any small object could be used. Examples: toothpicks, marshmallows, pictures cut from magazines, pennies, or colored papers.

2. **7-2-2A, 7-2-2B** Make the dice. Explain to the child that dice have dots on them that represent numbers. Tape the numbers 1 - 10 around the floor. Roll the dice and have the child count the dots. Then instruct the child to move to the number on the floor that represents the total number of dots on the dice.

3. Take an empty egg carton or muffin tin. Tape the numbers 1 - 10 on each slot. Instruct the child to fill each hole with the proper number of objects to correspond with each number. He could use macaroni, beans, pennies, etc.

4. **7-2-4** Make the spinner. Tape a sheet of paper with numbers 1 - 10 written in a vertical row on the floor. Have the child spin the spinner forward (clockwise) and move the number of spaces forward that the spinner points to. Next have him spin the spinner counter-clockwise and move backwards according to the number on the spinner.

5. **7-2-5** Instruct the child to complete the worksheet matching objects to numbers.

6. Instruct the child to make a number book. Let the child cut out objects and pictures from old magazines. Give the child ten pieces of blank paper with one of the numbers between 1 and 10 written at the top. Now have the child glue objects and pictures he has cut out on each sheet according to the number at the top. Example: If you have numbered the sheet three, then the child must glue any three things on that page. When the booklet is completed, have the child put the papers in order and staple it for him to make a neat number book.

7. For a special number treat, make the easy doughnuts found in the recipe section. Twist the doughnuts to form a figure "8" as shown in the diagram. Then cook according to directions.

Size
Lesson 3

Objectives

At the end of the lesson each child will be able to:

1. differentiate between small and large by putting things in sequence according to their size
2. differentiate between long and short by putting objects in sequence according to their length
3. name three living things that change size because they grow

Discussion

You (child) are bigger than some things and smaller than others. Your mother is bigger than you but you are bigger than a baby brother or sister. You are bigger than a toy car, but the car your mother drives is bigger than you.

Activities

1. Help the child find some things that are smaller than him. Some examples might be: dolls, toys, bug, younger brother or sister.
2. Now find some things that are larger than the child. Some examples might be: refridgerator, house, bed, car, Mother and Father.
3. **7-3-3** Tell the child the story of "The Three Bears." Then find the bowls, beds, and bears. Help the child paste the proper sized spoons and bowls with the right sized bear.

Discussion (continued)

Just as things are large and small, they are also short or long. Your Mother's legs are longer than your legs. Some carrots are long; some carrots are short.

Activities (continued)

4. Cut up a straw into several different-sized pieces; you could also use a piece of string. Hide the pieces in fairly obvious places around the room and let the child find them. When the pieces have all been found, help the child put them in order according to length.
5. **7-3-5** Make the giraffe whose neck grows longer and longer.

Discussion (continued)

Things that are alive do not always stay the same size. Kittens grow into bigger cats, puppies into dogs, calves into cows, and baby colts into horses. You change sizes too as you get older. The clothes that you wore last year or when you were a baby don't fit you anymore because you have grown bigger.

Some objects can also change sizes. If you stretch an elastic or blow up a balloon it will grow larger. An ice cube gets smaller as it melts. But these objects aren't alive like you and animals.

Activities (continued)

6. Have the child try on one of last year's outfits and discuss the places where the child has outgrown it. Look at baby pictures of the child and let him compare them to how he looks today.
7. Find pictures of baby and adult animals and show the child how they can grow and change size.
8. Make homemade bread or rolls using one of the recipes in the recipe section. Let the child look at the bread periodically and see how it rises and changes size.

Unit VIII
Health and Nutrition

Food For Life—Grain & Cereal Food Group Lesson 1

Objectives

At the end of the lesson each child will be able to:

1. tell one reason why our bodies need food
2. name at least one food that is from the grain and cereal food group

Discussion

Have you ever had hunger pains in your tummy? Hunger pains tell you it is time to fill your stomache with food. Any food will stop the hunger pains, but it is important that we eat the right kinds of foods that are best for our bodies. The body needs food for many reasons. The food we eat helps make heat to keep our bodies warm. Our bodies need fuel to run, just as a car needs gas. Food also helps our bodies stay in good working order. The more active we are, the more food our bodies need. When we are growing, like you are, our body especially needs good food to help us grow strong and healthy.

We all know that if we put water into the gas tank of our car instead of gas, it would not go. That isn't the right kind of fuel to make it function properly. We also need the right kind of fuel in our bodies to make them run properly. This fuel is called food, and it comes in what we call the four basic food groups. They are the grain and cereal group, meat group, milk group, and fruit and vegetable group. Today we are going to learn more about the grain and cereal group.

Activity

1. **8-1-1** Find the four basic food groups chart. Put it together and use it throughout this unit.

Discussion (continued)

Did you have toast or cereal for breakfast this morning? If you did, you had a food from the grain and cereal group. A grain is a seed that is grown in large grassy fields. The seed from the wheat plant is ground to make flour. Flour is used to make lots of good foods like bread, rolls, muffins, cake, cookies, and noodles.

Some other important grains are corn and rice. Corn can also be ground to make corn flour. It is used to make cereals such as Corn Chex, corn flakes, and breads such as corn bread.

Have you ever eaten rice with your dinner instead of a potato? In China and Japan, people eat rice at breakfast, lunch, and dinner.

Animals eat lots of grains. Horses love oats. Have you ever eaten oats? We eat oats in cooked oatmeal and oatmeal cookies. Oats, wheat, barley, rice, and corn are very nourishing foods that are rich in starch and protein. Grains and cereals help to give our bodies energy so we can run, skip, hop, jump, and play.

Activities (continued)

2. Cook some spaghetti noodles. Give each child several strands and let them make designs with it on a piece of paper. To make the noodles stick to the paper better, a little glue can be stirred into the noodles after they are cooked and drained. Kids love to do this!

3. **8-1-3** Find the chicken. Let the children glue rice, colored popcorn kernels, oats, and any other grains to fill in the chicken.
4. Let the children help you make oatmeal cookies. A super recipe is found in the recipe section.
5. Let each child make a cherrios or fruit loops necklace. String the cereal on some thread or string and tie the ends. They will love doing it and eating the finished product.
6. Let the children make Cinnamon Pinwheels or Orange Rolls found in the recipe section.
7. Read the story of the "Little Red Hen."
8. Let the children make cinnamon toast by simply sprinkling cinnamon on warm, buttered toast.

Milk Group
Lesson 2

Objectives

At the end of the lesson each child will be able to:

1. name one part of the body that milk is especially good for (bone, teeth)
2. name at least two products from the milk group

Discussion

The first food you were given after you were born was milk. Milk is especially good for babies and children that are growing every day like you, because it is rich in vitamins and minerals. Milk also supplies our bodies with *calcium*. Calcium is a hard word for you to say, but it is a very important thing, because it helps to build our bones and teeth.

You should have at least three servings of milk per day. Did you know that milk comes in many different foods? These foods are usually called dairy products. Can you name some? (butter, cheese, yogurt, ice cream, sour cream, cottage cheese) If you eat any of these foods, you are getting a serving of milk.

Where do these dairy products come from? Your mother probably bought them at the store, but they didn't make them at the store. First cows were fed the right kinds of food to produce good milk. The cows are milked twice a day, and then the milk is taken to a place where any harmful germs are killed that may have gotten into the milk. Then the milk is taken to a dairy where it is put into bottles and cartons and taken to the grocery store where you can buy it. The other dairy products such as butter, ice cream, and cottage cheese are made at the dairy from milk.

The body needs another liquid besides milk. This liquid is water. You need to drink four to six glasses of water a day. The water you drink replaces the water your body loses each day. Drinking water is very good for you, and it helps you keep your body in good working order.

Activities

1. Let the children try making their own butter. Put a small amount of cream in a baby jar. Instruct the child to shake it for a few minutes. It doesn't take very long until the cream starts to thicken and change to butter. A small amount of salt and yellow food coloring could be added. Let them eat their butter on pancakes or toast.
2. A simple Cheese Fondue recipe is included in the recipe section. Children really enjoy dipping pieces of French bread in it and eating this one.
3. **8-2-3** Instruct the child to complete the sequence worksheet on milk.
4. Make homemade ice cream. Recipe is found in the recipe section.
5. Let the children fix cottage cheese on crackers and eat them for a snack. Cream cheese or cheese spread could also be used.
6. Make the easy *American Cornstarch Pudding* in the recipe section.
7. **8-2-7** Find the worksheet on milk products and put it together.

Vegetables
Lesson 3

Objective

At the end of the lesson each child will be able to identify and name at least three vegetables.

Discussion

Vegetables are plants that are grown in the dirt or soil and used for food. The roots grow underneath the ground. Sometimes we eat only the roots of the vegetable or the part that grows under the ground. Some of these are *potatoes, yams, onions, and carrots.* Other vegetables we eat the part that grows above the ground, such as *lettuce, parsley, spinach, and cabbage.* Some vegetables grow on vines, such as *tomatoes, cucumbers, squash,* and *pumpkins.* Vegetables like peas and beans are really the seeds of the plants. Corn is probably the tallest vegetable in the garden because it grows on a cob in long stalks.

Have you ever heard the story of *Peter Rabbit?* (read the child the story; author is Beatrice Potter) Peter Rabbit kept sneaking into Mr. McGregor's garden, didn't he? Do you know why he went into the garden? Because he loved vegetables, and Mr. McGregor's garden had so many different and delicious vegetables. He had peas, spinach, potatoes, corn, tomatoes, lettuce, carrots, and cucumbers. One of Peter's favorite vegetables was cabbage. What is your favorite vegetable?

We need to eat vegetables every day, because they contain *vitamins* that will help us build strong bodies. Vegetables can be eaten and stored several different ways. Most vegetables can be eaten raw—this means without being cooked. Some vegetables are canned, and we heat them up before we eat them. Other vegetables can be frozen and we cook them before we eat them. Vegetables are sometimes cooked with other food groups. Many stews and spaghetti have meat and vegetables in them.

I hope you like vegetables as much as Peter Rabbit did, because they are so good for you. You need to have vegetables four times a day.

Activities

1. Visit a vegetable garden, if possible. If not, you could go to a grocery store or vegetable stand and look at the vegetables.
2. Make vegetable creatures—you will need:

several pieces and kinds of vegetables
knife
cutting board

Let each child sit around the kitchen bar or table. Cut up different vegetables and let them put the pieces together to form funny looking creatures.
3. Make one of the vegetable dips in the recipe section. Wash the vegetables the children have played with, and cut them into bite-sized pieces. Let them dip them into the dip and eat them.
4. **8-3-4** Instruct the child to make a vegetable creature.
5. Make a *Potato Necklace*—you will need:

several potatoes	knife
needle	potato peeler
coat thread	cutting board

Cut the potatoes into small cubes. Let each child string the cubes onto the coat thread. Separate the cubes slightly to allow air to get to all sides of each cube. Let the necklaces dry for a few days. Then let the child paint his necklace cubes with poster paint or magic marker.

6. **8-3-6** Instruct the child to do the worksheet on vegetable discrimination.
7. **8-3-7** Make peas in a pod.
8. Make a Rag Doll Salad as shown below. Children love this for lunch.

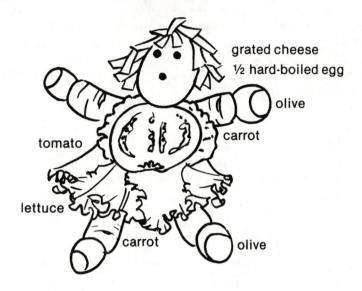

grated cheese
½ hard-boiled egg
olive
carrot
tomato
lettuce
carrot
olive

Fruit
Lesson 4

Objective

At the end of the lesson each child will be able to identify and name at least three fruits correctly.

Discussion

Fruits come in a variety of colors and flavors. Many fruits are sweet and some are sort of sour. Peaches, cherries, bananas, apples, and oranges are usually sweet. Grapefruit, lemons, and limes are usually sour. Have you ever noticed how many ice creams are fruit flavored? Can you name some? (Banana, strawberry, orange and lime sherbet, etc.)

Fruits grow on trees, shrubs, and vines. Bananas, peaches, cherries, plums, apricots, apples, and oranges are some of the fruits that grow on trees. Have you ever seen a fruit tree in bloom during spring? It has beautiful blossoms and flowers on it that give off a sweet fragrance like perfume. Grapes, watermelon, and cantelopes all grow on vines. We use purple grapes to make grape juice and grape jelly. Green grapes are fun to snack on and grow in clusters. Strawberries and other kinds of berries grow on short plants or shrubs. What is your favorite fruit to eat?

Activities

1. **8-4-1** Instruct the child to make the fruit tree.
2. Make a simple drawing of a tree. Let the child paste on popcorn or twisted pieces of pink crepe paper so the tree looks like it is in bloom.
3. Mix up some purple poster paint. Let each child dip their fingers in the paint and then press their finger on a plain piece of paper. Repeat the process to make a cluster of grapes.
4. Help the child make his own orange juice. Use a fruit juicer or a simple hand juicer would work.

Discussion (continued)

Fruit is not only delicious to eat, it is also very good for you. Citrus fruits like grapefruit, oranges, and lemons give us *Vitamin C.* Did you have a glass of orange juice or Tang for breakfast? If you did, you got your *Vitamin C* today. Vitamin C helps fight germs, especially those germs that make us get colds.

We usually harvest fruit in the late summer or fall. This is the time of year lots of parents are busy canning or freezing fruit that they can use for their families during the winter. Fruit can also be saved for a long time by drying it. Did you know that raisins are grapes that have been dried?

We make all kinds of things from fruit—juice, jam, jelly, cakes, pies. Fruit is so delicious, and fixed so many different ways, we can enjoy it all year long.

Activities (continued)

5. Cut many different fruits into bite-sized pieces. Make the chocolate fondue found in the recipe section. Let the children dip the fruit into the fondue using tooth picks.

6. Make a fruit candle that the child can eat. Put a half of a banana inside a piece of round sliced pineapple. Top with a cherry as shown.

7. Make the easy *Peach Cobbler* found in the recipe section. The children can help with this one.

Meat Group
Lesson 5

Objective

At the end of the lesson each child will be able to identify and name three products in the meat food group.

Discussion

The food we eat is put to work building tissue, keeping our bodies in good repair, and fighting off germs. Have you ever cut yourself or fallen down and scraped your knee? If your body did not build new tissue and repair, your cut would never get better. Can you imagine how many cuts you would still have if they hadn't healed and gone away. If our bodies didn't build new tissue, we wouldn't grow any bigger. That is why growing children like you need lots of protein to grow hair, bones, teeth, and muscles.

We get protein from eating certain foods. The foods that give us the most protein per serving are found in the meat group. What are some meat and fish that you like to eat at meal time? (bacon, hamburger, chicken, turkey, tuna, etc.) Chickens give us eggs; cows give us hamburger; pigs give us ham and bacon. Nuts are also a very high source of protein. I'm sure most of you have eaten peanut butter sandwiches or cookies. Have you ever eaten any other kind of nut? We also can get protein from eating beans. We usually eat beans in things like chili and baked beans

Each one of you needs at least two servings of protein a day. Most of the foods we eat are a combination of the four food groups we have talked about. Vegetable soup can have meat, noodles (grain), and vegetables in it. Macaroni and cheese has milk, butter, cheese, and noodles in it. When we eat a tuna fish sandwich for lunch, we are getting bread (cereal group), butter (milk group), and tuna (meat group). Eating properly is so important for a growing body like yours, so remember to eat the foods that are good for you so you can grow up to be strong and healthy.

Activities

1. Let the child help you make individual foil dinners to bake in the oven. Cut up some potatoes and carrots and onions. Mix them together and put a serving on a piece of foil wrap. Now add a small hamburger patti and salt and pepper to taste. Wrap the foil around the hamburger and vegetables. Place the dinners on a cookie sheet and bake at 350° for 45 minutes.
2. **8-5-2** Instruct the child to complete the worksheet on animals and the food they give us.
3. Mix up a batch of peanut butter playdough using the recipe in the recipe section. Let the children pretend to make the different animals and cuts of meat we get from them. If the children wash their hands before they start, this kind of playdough is edible.
4. Other food suggestions for this day might be to make corn dogs or deviled eggs. Recipes can be found in the recipe section.
5. Let the children make a turtle or mouse out of walnut shells as shown in the diagram below. Break the walnut in half and shell it. Cut pieces of felt for the head, eyes, nose, and tail. Paint the shells, if you desire. Glue the felt in the proper places.

6. Make a bean bag out of an old sock. Simply fill the sock with beans and tie the opening shut. You could cut off both ends and sew them after you have filled the sock with beans to make a square bean bag.

Sleep
Lesson 6

Objective

At the end of the lesson each child will be able to tell at least one reason why sleep is important to our bodies.

Discussion

Growing is the most important thing your body does. We can tell we are growing when we are measured and weighed from time to time. Regular growth is the first sign of a healthy child. There are several things that help you grow: (1) eat proper foods, (2) keep your body clean, (3) get plenty of sleep, (4) exercise. A growing child like you needs lots of sleep. You should go to bed at a regular time each night and sleep for 10 - 12 hours. When you do not get enough sleep, you feel tired and cross.

You grow faster when you are asleep than when you are awake because you are not using energy for work and play when you are asleep. Growing children usually stretch and roll around in their sleep. Do you ever kick your blankets off without knowing it?

Activity

1. Let each child lay down and pretend he is asleep. Instruct the child to roll over and stretch with his eyes closed.

Discussion (continued)

It is good to have a quiet activity before going to bed, like story time, reading a book, or listening to some soft music. It is much harder to go to sleep if you have been playing hard right before you go to bed.

When you get ready to go to bed, you need to put on your pajamas. If your pajamas are clean and fresh, and if you have had a bath or shower, you will sleep much better. Make sure your pajamas are not too tight, and that you have just enough covers to keep you comfortable.

Most babies learn to sleep in the dark. Sleeping without a light on is a good, healthy habit. You feel more rested and your eyes are less tired when the light is off.

Sleep keeps you well and healthy so you can fight off germs and grow properly.

Activities (continued)

2. **8-6-2** Help the child put the day and night pictures together.
3. **8-6-3A, 8-6-3B** Dress the three bears in their pajamas and put them in the proper sized beds.
4. **8-6-4** Make the sleepy person.

Cleanliness and Good Grooming
Lesson 7

Objective

At the end of the lesson each child will be able to name at least three things we need to do each day to keep ourselves clean and well-groomed.

Discussion

The outside of our bodies is covered with skin. Skin helps protect our bodies. All over our skin are tiny openings called pores. Have you ever played really hard and gotten hot and sweaty? When the body gets warm, it perspires or sweats. Tiny beads of water come out of the pores in our skin. Sometimes when we play, we also get very dirty. What can we do to get rid of the dirt and perspiration on our bodies? A bath or a shower in warm, soapy water will wash away the dirt and perspiration, won't it? When you are clean you look better and feel better. When we take a bath, we need to make sure we scrub all parts of our body. Don't forget your ears, face, and neck; these places are easier to get clean if you use a wash cloth.

When you are through with your bath, always put on clean underwear, clothes, or pajamas. You will want your clothing to be as fresh and clean as you are.

Taking good care of your clothes is important. Do you put your soiled clothes in the laundry basket instead of back in your drawers? When you have dressed up in your nicer clothes for church or a special activity, always remember to change back into your play clothes when you get home. If we take good care of our clothes and make sure they are washed when needed, we will look nicer and feel better about ourselves.

To go along with our clean body and clean clothes, we need to have a clean mouth. Brush your teeth often—at least twice a day and usually after you have eaten. Our hands need to be washed many times a day, too. You should wash them before you eat and after you use the restroom.

Activities

1. Let the child pretend he is in the bath tub washing himself. You could let him use a dry wash cloth to clean behind his ears, etc.
2. **8-7-2** Instruct the child to complete the *Rub-a-Dub Three Men in a Tub.*
3. **8-7-3** Help the child put together the cleanliness chart.
4. **8-7-4** Help the child find what is wrong with the grooming of the children in the picture.
5. Let the child make soap balls out of soap flakes or *Ivory* soap. Add water and food coloring to soap flakes and form in a ball; let dry.

Germs
Lesson 8

Objective

At the end of the lesson each child will be able to name three ways in which he can prevent the spreading of germs.

Discussion

Did you know there are tiny plants that grow all around us where they are not wanted? These plants are called germs. Long ago people didn't know there were such things as germs, because they are so small we can't see them. One day a man was looking through a microscope. A microscope is a machine that makes things look larger. (show children a microscope or a magnifying glass) The man saw tiny, living things moving around that were later called germs.

Germs are everywhere. They are in the air you breathe, on your hands, and even in your mouth and body. Not all germs are harmful, and many of them will never bother us if we use good cleanliness habits.

Germs grow in many places. They grow very fast in warm, moist places. Can you think of a place in your body that germs might want to grow? Germs grow easily in your mouth, because it is warm and moist. That is why we should never put things besides clean food in our mouths, such as pencils, fingers, toys, etc. Germs are always on our fingers and other objects and can get into our mouths easily. That is why we need to wash our hands before we eat, after we play outside, and after we use the restroom. We must also make sure our fingernails are clean, because germs can grow under them.

There are several ways to keep germs out of our mouths. Use only your own toothbrush; always drink from a clean glass; always eat with a clean knife, fork or spoon, and plate; don't touch your mouth on any part of a public drinking fountain.

Activity

1. Peel a potato and cut it in half. Rinse off one half of the potato and place it in a clean, glass jar with a lid. Give the child the other half of potato and let him handle it and breathe on it. Now put the other half in a clean jar with a lid. In a few days the child will be able to see how the germs have grown. Make sure you label each bottle so you know which is the clean and which is the germy potato.

Discussion (continued)

Many diseases are carried from one person to another. If someone is careless, he can give us his germs. What should we do when we cough or sneeze? We need to cover our mouths so we don't spread our germs. We need to stay away from someone who is sick. If you are sick, where should you stay? (at home) Do not play with your friends or brothers and sisters until you are better.

Today we are protected from many diseases that long ago people died from. When you were a baby you were vaccinated; that means you were given a shot or some medicine that would protect you from getting many bad diseases. Before children can go to school, they must be vaccinated against several diseases. What would happen if children weren't vaccinated? We would not be protected from many diseases, would we?

All of us have cut or hurt ourselves at one time or another. The important thing to remember is that if we get a cut or hurt, we must wash it so germs won't grow and cause it to hurt more. Sometimes our parents will wash our hurts off with a soft cotton ball. When your cut is clean, your parents will probably put a little medicine on it and then cover it with a bandaid so more germs cannot get into it.

Activities (continued)

2. Let the children help you wash any washable toys to get the germs off of them. You could get an assembly line going at the kitchen sink or, if it is warm, you could wash them out on the lawn with a garden hose.

3. **8-8-3** Let the child repair the injured girl with bandaids.

4. Put some cotton balls in a sack or bottle with some dry tempera paint. Shake until the cotton balls are colored. Let each child make a picture with the cotton balls by rubbing them on a paper or gluing them to a paper. Spray with hair spray when finished to keep the paint from spreading around.

Unit IX
Transportation Unit

Early Transportation
Lesson 1

Objectives

At the end of the lesson each child will be able to:

1. tell what transportation means
2. name two kinds of early transportation

Discussion

Transportation refers to various systems or methods of moving people, animals, or things from place to place. Many years ago, man had no way of going from place to place but to walk. He carried his belongings on his back, heads, and arms. He learned to carry his things in a pack. Then man invented a "skid." This was two long poles parallel to each other with animal skin stretched across and attached to each pole. It resembled our modern-day stretcher. Man could then put heavy things on the skid and carry them.

Activities

1. Have the child skip, walk, and run. Point out to him that his feet are one way of transportation.
2. Make a "skid" by taking two straws or small sticks and using a scrap of material in place of an animal skin. Stretch the material between the two straws and attach it with string, glue or staples. Let the child carry beans, marshmallows, or toothpicks on it.

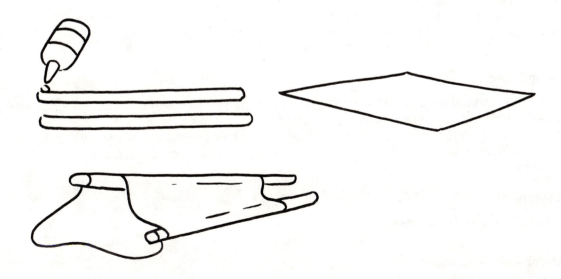

Discussion

Man soon found that certain animals could be tamed and used for riding and carrying things. They learned to ride horses, camels, and elephants. These animals are still used today for transportation and recreation.

Activities (continued)

3. **9-1-3** Instruct the child to complete the worksheet on animals.
4. Visit a zoo; particularly see those animals that were used for early transportation.

Wheels
Lesson 2

Objectives

At the end of the lesson each child will be able to:

1. tell why we use wheels
2. name three transportation vehicles that have wheels

Discussion

Man found that it was easier to roll a log than to drag it. He began to make wheels from the round trunk of a tree. The wheels early man made from trees were very heavy and rolled slowly, so man took out the center and put spokes inside. They moved much easier and faster.

Activities

1. Bring together a group of objects. Have the child examine them and determine whether they can roll like a wheel. Examples: egg, coin, log-shaped sticks, orange, apple, toy wheel, ring, glass; things that don't roll: fork, piece of bread, book, toothbrush, shoe.
2. Show the child the wheels on a bike and any other vehicles close by that he can examine.
3. Make a special wheel treat out of caramel corn using the recipe in the recipe section. Form the caramel corn into the shape of a wheel. Stick thin licorice strings on for spokes.

Discussion (continued)

One of the first kinds of transportation vehicles used by people to travel and haul things in was a wagon. The early pioneers traveled in covered wagons pulled by horses and oxen.

Eventually someone built an engine that could be run by using gasoline. A car with this type of engine was called the "horseless carriage." Today we have all sorts of cars, trucks, and buses that have wheels and are run on gasoline.

Activities (continued)

4. Make a covered wagon. You will need:

shoe box	tape
construction paper	scissors
bracket	glue
string	

Cut four wheels out of construction paper and attach them in the appropriate places by using brackets or glue. Take a sheet of construction paper (8½" x 11") and curve it over the top of the shoe box for a cover. Attach it on the sides with masking tape. A string could also be attached in front so the child can pull it around the room.

5. Instruct the child to look through some old magazines and find pictures of trucks, cars, and busses. Have him paste them on a piece of paper.

6. **9-2-6A, 9-2-6B** Cut out the car and truck. Pull them along the road as shown.

7. **9-2-7** Make a license plate for the child's bike. Cover it with Saran Wrap or have it laminated in plastic. Attach it to the child's bike using a shoe lace, string, or wire.

8. *P.E. suggestion for today:* ride a bike or bounce up and down on an old inner tube.

Water Travel
Lesson 3

Objectives

At the end of the lesson each child will be able to:

1. tell two reasons why people started using water as a means of transportation
2. name two kinds of ships

Discussion

People had to cross streams and rivers to look for food or new places to live. They could wade across some streams and swim, but they could not carry things. Many noticed that a log didn't sink but floated in the water. So they tied several logs together to make a raft. This way people could ride on the raft and carry goods back and forth across the river. Next people started making canoes out of tree trunks. It was hard to push and pull the boat through the water, so sails were used, and the wind helped push the boat. Oars were used to steer and help move the boat in the water.

Activities

1. Try different objects in the sink or bathtub and see if they float. Have the child try such things as a cork, coin, comb, sponge, ball, toy boat, leaf, or piece of wood.

2. Make a raft out of straws or popsicle sticks and float it in the water. Make it similar to the diagram below.

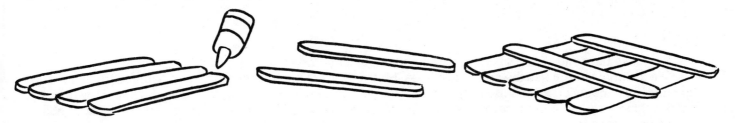

3. Make a soap boat. Poke a popsicle stick through a 3" x 3" piece of paper for a sail. Then poke the stick into a cake of ivory soap. Float the soap boat in a tub or sink.

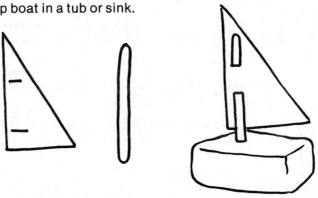

Discussion

Today we have steam ships. Ships are used to carry goods. These goods are called cargo. There are two kinds of ships: freighters and tankers. Freighters carry dry cargo such as wheat, corn, and spices. Tankers carry liquid cargo such as gasoline and oil. Big ocean ships that carry people are called liners. They are like hotels on water. They have dining rooms, libraries, shops, swimming pools, movie threaters, and game rooms. Some are as long as two city blocks. Smaller boats give us recreational fun. We use them for water skiing, fishing, and sailing.

Activitiy (continued)

4. **9-3-4** Instruct the child to do the worksheet concerning small and large concept.

Trains
Lesson 4

Objectives

At the end of the lesson each child will be able to:

1. name two types of trains and what each transports
2. name two workers on the train and one of their duties

Discussion

The first railroad car in the country was pulled by a horse. Then they invented steam engines. Steam engines run by coal. At first men had to shovel coal into the firebox; now an automatic shoveler shoots the coal in.

Today many locomotives or trains are diesel electric and burn oil instead of coal. These trains made transportation for man a lot faster and they could also carry a lot of freight and goods.

There are different kinds of trains. A freight train carries supplies and food such as pigs, horses, fuel, and wood. The commuter train takes people to and from work in the larger cities. A pullman train travels long distances. It has a restaurant, where people can eat, and sleeping compartments.

A conductor is a very vital person on the train. He wears a special badge on his coat and takes people's tickets. He also signals the engineer with a special lantern. He is responsible for the train moving exactly at the right time. There are a lot of trains and just a few tracks. If they get mixed up they might crash into each other.

The engineer is the person who drives the train. He sits in the engine cab on the right side so he can lean out the window and see everything on the tracks.

Activities

1. **9-4-1** Make the conductor's badge. Color it and let the child wear it.
2. Make a signal lantern like the conductor uses. Fold a 9″ x 12″ piece of construction paper lengthwise. Have the child make many cuts from the fold to approximately one inch from the edge. Open the paper, overlapping the two 9-inch edges, and paste or staple them together. A strip handle from the same color paper can be pasted across the top.

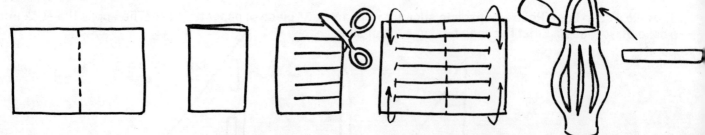

3. **9-4-3** Find the conductor's watch. Make a paper chain and attach it to the watch.
4. **9-4-4** Make the engineer's hat.

Flying Things
Lesson 5

Objectives

At the end of the lesson each child will be able to:

1. name two flying things used for transportation
2. name one reason why flying is a good method of transportation

Discussion

We need all kinds of transportation to carry people and things from place to place. Trains and cars are fine for traveling on the land, but we need another kind of transportation that can fly over the big oceans to other countries and far away places. That is why airplanes are such a good kind of transportation. They are also very fast—much faster than cars, trains, or ships.

Throughout time, people have wanted to fly like the birds in the sky. The first flying machine was a balloon filled with warm air. It would go where the wind blew it. A basket was attached on the end of the balloon and people could ride inside it.

Wilbur and Orville Wright were two brothers who worked very hard to build an airplane. They used gasoline to keep the motor going and were successful in flying the first airplane.

Today many people travel on airplanes. We go to airports to fly on airplanes. Pilots drive the airplanes and helicopters. A rocket is another flying machine that is much faster than an airplane. Astronauts fly rockets and have even flown as far as the moon.

Activities

1. Blow up a balloon with air and see how it floats in the sky. A helium filled balloon would even better demonstrate this principle.
2. **9-5-2** Make the fun flying toys.
3. **9-5-3A** Play the transportation game.
   9-5-3B Movers for transportation game.

Unit X
Animals

Animals and Their Noses
Lesson 1

Objectives

At the end of the lesson each child will be able to:

1. name three animals and match their noses with the correct body when asked
2. tell three things animals use their noses for

Discussion

An animal is any living thing that can move about on its own, but is unable to make its own food. Animals seem to be everywhere. Many people have pet animals such as dogs and cats. There are also animals at the zoo, the circus, under the water and in the air.

Animals are a lot like people. Many animals have eyes, ears, nose, mouth, arms, and legs like we do. Of course, the animal's parts look very different from ours. In fact, animals look different from one another because their body parts are different. An animal's body parts are sometimes very special, because they help him take care of his needs.

People smell and breathe with their noses. But for many animals, their noses have many other uses. The elephant has a very special nose. He not only uses it to smell, but he can use it to pick up things like we use our hands. He can pick up food to eat or sticks to play with. He can also suck up water and either store it in his nose or spray it like a shower. We call an elephant's nose a trunk.

Activities

1. Find several pictures of animals in books and magazines. Show them to the child and have him point out to you the different body parts such as arms, legs, eyes, ears, mouth, and nose.
2. **10-1-2** Make the elephant head and trunk. Thread the straw through the trunk and let the child drink out of it.

Discussion (continued)

Rhinoceros' and alligators are in water a lot. When they go under the water to swim and find food, their noses close up to keep out the water.

Fish have noses too, but they don't use them for breathing. They have special gills on the sides of their face that they breath through. This way they can get air in the water and not have to come out of the water to breath.

A pig's nose has a small barb on the end of it that he can use to dig in the mud for food.

Activities (continued)

3. **10-1-3** Complete the unfinished pictures of animals on the worksheet. Paste the correct animal's nose on the body.

4. Make a marshmallow pig using a large marshmallow for the body and miniature marshmallows for the feet, ears, nose, and tail. The child can stick them together by licking the small marshmallows and then putting them in place. Each child can then eat his own pig.

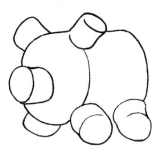

Animal Ears and Feet
Lesson 2

Objectives

At the end of the lesson each child will be able to:

1. name three things animals use their feet for
2. match three animals' feet and lower body with the animals' ears and top of body correctly

Discussion

Most animals have ears that help him hear just like we do. You can often tell an animal simply by the shape of his ears. A rabbit has large, long, floppy ears; a cat has pointed erect ears; a bear has small, round ears.

Activities

1. Using the same pictures you did for the previous lesson, point out the ears of several animals. Have each child look at his own ears in a mirror and compare them with the shape of animal ears.

2. **10-2-2** Make an animal hat. This same pattern can be used to make a rabbit, bear, or cat simply by changing the ears. Make the hat out of construction paper and follow the diagram and instructions below.

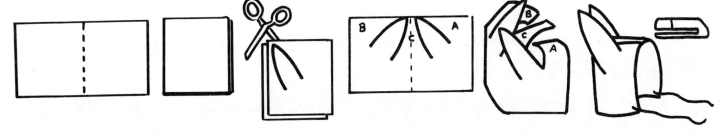

Using an 11″ × 17″ sheet of paper (or two 8½″ × 11″ stapled together), fold in half to 8½″ × 11″, place pattern of ears over the folded sheet so that the desired ear is flush with the edge of the folded paper. Cut out desired shape. Open the folded paper and bend C section forward. Holding C section in place, bend section A and B underneath C and overlap A and B until the hat is formed. Staple A, B and C together on front edge. Attach yarn or string at bottom corners for ties.

Discussion (continued)

Many animals have special feet that they use for other things besides walking. The bear, cat, and lion have claws on their feet. These claws help them to dig in the ground, to climb trees, and to eat their food. A bat's feet are hooked to his wings and are also like a claw. He uses his feet to hang upside down on the limb of a tree. Some animals have webbed feet like ducks and penguins. Their webbed feet help them to swim in the lakes and rivers. Horses, goats, sheep, and cows have special feet called hooves. It almost looks like they are wearing a pair of shoes, because they don't have toes like many other animals.

Activities (continued)

3. **10-2-3** Find the worksheet regarding animal feet.
4. **10-2-4A, 10-2-4B** Cut out the animal cards. Help the child match the cards correctly. Later, he can mix up the cards to make funny animals.

Animal Tails
Lesson 3

Objective

At the end of the lesson each child will be able to:

1. match three animals bodies with their correct tail
2. name three ways animals use their tails to help them

Discussion

Unlike people, most animals have a tail. A tail is the part of the body that sticks out from the animal's back end. An animal's tail can be very helpful. Horses and cows use their tails like a whip to chase away mosquitoes and black flies. A beaver uses his tail like a rudder or an oar to help him move and swim through the water. He also uses it to slap the water to warn the other beavers of danger. When a skunk raises his black and white tail—run! He sprays a stinky scent six to eight feet in order to protect himself from anything that might harm him. An anteater has a bushy tail. When it rains he uses it like an umbrella to keep himself dry. Monkeys have long tails. They use them to pick up things or hang from branches and swing back and forth. When a dog wags his tail we know he is excited and happy to see us.

Activities

1. **10-3-1** Cut out the animals and tails. Let the child color the animals and then paste the correct tail on the animals.
2. **10-3-2** Make the dog with the wagging tail.

Animal Coverings
Lesson 4

Objective

At the end of the lesson each child will be able to name three types of covering animals have.

Discussion

People have skin and hair to cover their bodies. Animals also have many types of coverings to keep them warm and give them protection. Cats, dogs, and bears are just a few animals that have fur on their bodies to keep them warm. A cat's fur becomes softer and silkier when it is a household pet. Horses, lions, and cats have a mane or ruff on their necks that frames their faces.

Activities

1. **10-4-1** Find the cat. Make whiskers and attach where slotted and then cover its body with pulled-apart cotton balls. Glue them on with Elmer's or school glue. The cotton balls can be easily colored by putting them in a paper sack with dry tempra paints and shaking.
2. Make a lion face with a mane. Cut out three circles of yellow, orange, and brown construction paper the same size of a paper plate. Trace around the paper plate; cut out the circles. Place the circles on top of each other and staple them in the center. Then have the child draw around a smaller object approximately 40″ in diameter to form a face in the middle of the top circle. Have the child cut all three pieces of paper at once from the outside of the circle to the edge of the smaller circle, making fringe. Instruct the child to curl the three colors of fringe by rolling it on a pencil or on his fingers to form the lion's mane. Complete the animal by drawing facial features with crayons. The lion can be suspended as a mobile.

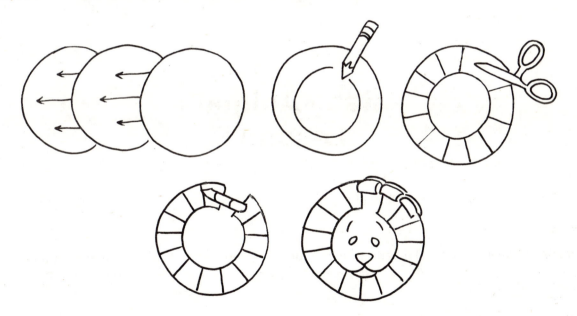

Discussion (continued)

Birds have feathers to control body temperature and keep them comfortable in all kinds of weather. Fish have scales all over their slippery bodies. The porcupine is covered with quills on its back and sides. These quills are a porcupine's protection. The quills have sharp ends with barbs on the end that stick into anything when released. Clams, snails, oysters, crayfish, and lobsters have a shell covering. Frogs, toads, and salamanders have a slimy smooth skin.

Activities (continued)

3. Make a clam shell and snail drawing by tracing your hands as shown below.

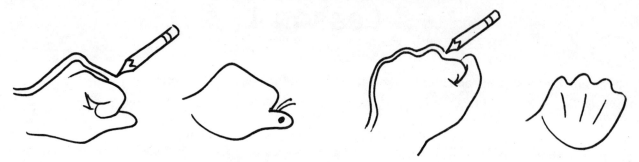

4. Make a potato porcupine. Stick toothpicks into a potato all around the sides and top. Use cloves for the eyes and nose.

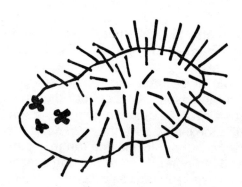

Baby Animals
Lesson 5

Objective

At the end of the lesson each child will be able to identify and properly name four baby animals.

Discussion

Animals have babies and take care of them much like people do. Animal babies have special names. A baby cat is a kitten; a dog is a puppy; a sheep a lamb; a goat a kid; a cow a calf; a lion a cub; a horse a colt; and a baby rabbit is called a bunny.

Activities

1. **10-5-1** Do the worksheet. Match the baby animal with its mother.
2. **10-5-2** Cut out the mother rabbit and her bunnies.

Discussion (continued)

When people have babies we usually have them one at a time or sometimes two at a time, which is called twins. It is very unusual for a person to have 3, 4, 5, or 6 babies at a time, but it is not uncommon for many animals to have that many babies at one time. When an animal has 3, 4, 5, 6 or more babies at a time, it is called a litter. Pigs, cats, dogs, and rabbits usually have their babies in litters. A bear usually has two cubs at a time. A cow, horse, lamb, or goat usually has one baby or twins. Chickens, birds, fish, and turtles lay eggs. After a certain length of time, the babies hatch out of the egg shell.

Activities (continued)

3. If possible, visit a nearby farm where the children can see a litter of animals or any mother with her babies. A pet store often has a litter of rabbits, hamsters, or puppies that you could go visit.
4. **10-5-4** Make the stand-up folded mother pig and babies.

Discussion (continued)

People carry their babies around in their arms when they are small. Most animals use their arms for walking, so they have to carry their babies in different ways. Dogs and cats carry their babies by taking hold of the extra fur around the baby's neck with their teeth.

A kangaroo carries its baby in a special pouch. The baby stays there for the first four months of its life. The baby gets his milk while in the pouch.

A baby cow (calf), baby horse(colt), baby elephant, and baby giraffe are just some of the animals that are too big when they are born to be carried by their mothers. They learn to stand and walk very soon after their birth.

Activity (continued)

5. **10-5-5** Make the kangaroo-in-a-pouch.

Animal Homes On and Above the Ground
Lesson 6

Objectives

At the end of the lesson each child will be able to:

1. name two places animals make their homes at ground level
2. name two places animals make their homes above the ground

Discussion

Just like people, animals need somewhere to live to give them shelter from their surroundings. Some animals build their homes on top of the ground. A rabbit builds his nest in fields. He makes it out of soft grass and lines it with fur. The mother rabbit uses her own fur to line the nest. A fox finds a hollow log or a hole among the rocks to make his home. A garden spider lives in a garden among the plants. The spider weaves a web and usually stays on or near his web.

Activities

1. Make a black spider by cutting a circle of any size out of construction paper. Make one cut through the circle to the center. Overlap the cut to give the circle a coned effect and tape it. Cut six narrow strips of paper for the spider's legs and crinkle them. Paste the legs around the circle. Take a string up through the center and hang it where the child requests.
2. Make the special "Bunny and Jello" treat using the recipe found in the recipe section.

Discussion (continued)

Many other animals build their homes above the ground. Squirrels build their homes in the branches of a tree. In the winter squirrels move inside a hole in the tree. Racoons live in hollow trees near the water. They wash all of their food before they eat it. Birds build their nests high in trees or bushes. Sometimes they will even build a nest under the eaves of houses, barns, or other buildings. Birds build their nests out of bits of string, twigs, leaves, and other small things that they find on the ground.

Bees live with many other bees in a group called a "swarm". They make their home in hollow trees or a hive. Bees fill their homes with honey comb, which is wax made by the bees. The bees also make honey and store it in the wax honey comb rooms in the hive.

Activities (continued)

3. **10-6-3** Find the tree and match the animals with their homes.
4. Make a nest out of clay or playdough. Help the child roll long, narrow strips of clay and layer them in a circular stack for the nest. Then make little round bits of clay for eggs and place them in the nest.
5. Buy a piece of honey comb and let the child examine the wax and taste the honey.
6. Make peanut butter and honey sandwiches for lunch.

Animal Homes Underground
Lesson 7

Objective

At the end of the lesson each child will be able to name two animals that make their homes under the ground.

Discussion

Some animals make their homes under the ground, much like if they were living in a basement. The woodchuck makes two doors to his home. If an enemy comes in one door, he can run out the other.

The ground squirrel leaves a pile of dirt outside his door. The chipmunk makes tunnels and special rooms to store things in his home underground.

The skunk most often makes his home underground. He does not dig his own home. He uses holes that other animals have made and left.

The ant digs a hole in the ground under a log or rock. They make lots of tunnels or halls. At the end of each tunnel is a room. Many of the rooms are used to store food.

Activities

1. Go on a nature walk. Look in fields for any signs of underground animals. Let the child guess what animal might be living in any hole that you might find.
2. **10-7-2** Do the worksheet animal maze.

Discussion (continued)

The beaver builds his home out of logs, twigs, branches, and stones. He gnaws down trees with his sharp teeth and builds a dam across a creek with the fallen tree logs. The dam stops the water from running down the creek and it spreads out into a pond. After the dam is built, the beavers build their home. It is located above the water, but the door is under the water. The beavers store extra logs under the water for food; they eat the bark.

Water Animals
Lesson 8

Objective

At the end of the lesson each child will be able to name two animals that make their homes in the water.

Discussion

Frogs live in ponds, but they can also move and hop on the ground. When frogs were babies they looked much like a tiny fish. But as they got older they grew arms and legs and learned to hop out of the water onto land. They can still swim in the water but can search for food on the land if they need to.

Turtles also like to swim, but they live on land also. Turtles walk very slowly and carry a special home on their backs called a shell. If a turtle wants to hide, he can just pull his head, legs, and arms inside the shell and hold very still.

Activities

1. **10-8-1** For a fun racing game, make the jumping frog and slow turtle.
2. Make a frog by cutting two circles out of green construction paper approximately 4″ in diameter. Fold one of the circles in half. Cut the other circle in half and paste the two halves on the other circle so that the straight openings face the fold in the circle. This will make two pockets for the child's hand to open and shut the frog's mouth. Cut two arms and two legs and paste them in the appropriate places on the frog. Draw eyes to complete the frog.

3. Make a turtle by using a small paper plate as the turtle's shell. Instruct the child to paint or color the back of the plate. Make the turtle's neck and head by fan-folding a strip of paper as shown below. Poke it through a slit in one end of the paper plate and paste the end of it to the unpainted side of the plate. Paste a construction paper head to the other end of the fan-folded strip. Paste a small paper tail to the unpainted side so it sticks out from the other end of the plate. To form the legs, cut four strips of construction paper about 1″ x 4″ long. Roll one end around a pencil and paste it to form a foot. Attach the feet under the plate with tape or a stapler.

4. Make "chocolate turtles" found in the recipe section.

Discussion (continued)

Fish live in oceans, rivers, lakes, streams, or ponds. They have special bodies that enable them to live in the water all the time. They have gills that let them breathe while in the water. Fish have fins that they use to help them move through the water. People don't have fins, so we use our arms and legs to help us swim through the water.

Fish come in all different sizes. Some large fish are sharks, whales, tuna, and salmon. Some small fish are gold fish and guppies. The very small fish we can keep in aquariums so we can watch and enjoy them. Fish give us food and they also help us by eating insects like mosquitos.

Activities (continued)

5. Instruct the child to "play fish" in the tub or swimming pool. Have him try kicking his legs and feet and holding his legs and ankles together at the same time. (This could also be done on the floor.)
6. **10-8-6** Make the pull fish.
7. Let the child play like he is going fishing. Make a fishing pole out of a long stick and a piece of string attached at the end. Make some simple fish out of construction paper in various sizes. Put all of the fish into a bowl and let the child fish for them. Clip a fish onto his pole with a paper clip. When all of the fish have been caught, help the child put them in the proper order according to size.
8. Have tuna fish sandwiches for lunch.
9. Make an aquarium out of a shoe box. Paint the box blue inside or cover the inside with light blue construction paper. Turn the box on its side so that the bottom is now one of the sides of the box. Make small colored fish out of construction paper. Attach a short string to each fish and suspend them in the box by taping the string to the top. (see diagram) Paste small pebbles or colored, smashed macaroni on the bottom of the box. Cover the front of the box (open end) with plastic wrap. Look in at the fish like you would an aquarium.

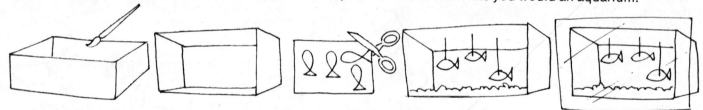

Animal Pets
Lesson 9

Objective

At the end of the lesson each child will be able to name three pets that can live in our home or yard.

Discussion

Animals that are tame and can live with us in our homes or yard are called pets. A pet could be a dog, cat, fish, bird, box turtle, guinea pig, or hamster.

Have you ever gone to a pet store? If you look into the pet store windows, you can see all kinds of fun pets you might like. We can just look at all the pets in a pet store, but if we have a pet of our own we need to take care of it. Pets require special food and lots of love. They need to sleep and get exercise like we do. It is important to be careful when handling a pet. We need to make sure we don't hurt them when we pick them up or pet them. You can hug some pets (dog, cat) but you must be gentle.

Activities

1. Get a stuffed animal and let the child practice petting it and holding it correctly. If a baby kitty or puppy is near by, then let him try holding and petting a live pet.
2. Make a pet store window. Cut four strips of black construction paper. Make two of the strips 8½" long and two 11" long. Paste the strips on a piece of white paper in a "tick, tac, toe" formation. In each square, instruct the child to draw one of his favorite animals inside.
3. Visit your local pet store and let the child see the different animals that could be pets.

Discussion (continued)

Many pets can eat table scraps that we leave, but there are also special foods for our pets. You can buy canned or dry food for your cat or dog. Cats also need and like to drink milk. Guinea pigs, gerbils, and rabbits like lettuce, vegetables, bread crust, and apples. Birds eat bird seed, bugs, insects, or bread crumbs.

Our pets need a certain spot that they know is their own to sleep. This could be either in our homes or yard, depending on the pet. A canary or parakeet bird would need a bird cage. A gerbil or hamster would also need a cage so it wouldn't run away. Dogs and cats need to have a special basket or box with a soft blanket on the bottom. Some bigger dogs have their own dog house or kennel outside.

Whatever pet we have, we must learn to take care of its needs. That way, you will have a happy pet and he will be a friend to you for a long time.

Activities (continued)

4. **10-9-4** Do the worksheet on pets and their homes.
5. **10-9-5** Make a mask of your favorite pet.

Farm Animals
Lesson 10

Objective

At the end of the lesson each child will be able to name three animals that we find on the farm.

Discussion

Another place we find animals is on a farm. Can you name some animals that make their home on the farm? (chickens, cows, horses, goats, turkeys, sheep, pigs, rabbits)

The farmer raises most of these animals to provide food for us. We get beef and milk from cows, bacon from pigs, eggs from chickens, wool from sheep, and our Thanksgiving dinner from the turkey.

Horses can oftentimes help the farmer with his work. They can pull heavy things and help the farmer round-up his cattle or sheep. Horses are also fun to ride through the fields or down a country lane.

Activities

1. **10-10-1** Sing the song "Old McDonald Had a Farm." Animals are included in packet to hold up during song.
2. Make farm animals out of clay. You could use one of the clay recipes in the recipe section. Many different animals can be made by simply forming a piece of clay in the shape of a horse shoe for the body and then adding a simple head, tail, and ears.

Discussion (continued)

A cow is not the only farm animal from which we get milk. Goats' milk can also be very delicious. Pigs, sheep, chickens, turkeys, and cows all give us food to eat, but the sheep and cow also give us clothing. The sheep's fur is sheared off in the spring and made into beautiful wool sweaters and other articles of clothing. Wool clothing is very warm. Cow hides (skins) are very strong and are used to make leather coats, purses, shoes, and belts.

Farm animals need a place to sleep and to keep warm, so they have their own house. It is called a barn. Animals love to be outside, but when it rains or is cold, the animals go into the barn.

The farmer not only provides a home for his farm animals, but he spends time each day feeding them. The cattle and sheep eat grass and hay. Chickens have special feed made of different grains. Horses like oats and barley. The farmer must also milk the cows two times a day (once in the morning and once at night) and gather the eggs that the chickens have laid.

Activities (continued)

3. **10-10-3A, 10-10-3B, 10-10-3C** Cut out the barn and farm animals. Follow the instructions for putting the barn together.
4. Play and sing "Farmer in the Dell" found in music section.
5. Play "Farm" found in the P. E. unit.

Zoo and Wild Animals
Lesson 11

Objective

At the end of the lesson each child will be able to name three animals that are found in the zoo.

Discussion

Wild animals that would be too dangerous to have as pets live in many different places . . . the desert, jungle, forest, and mountains. It would be frightening to meet up with a ferocious lion in the jungle, but chances are you don't live by a jungle. We have zoos so we can see these kinds of wild animals. Animals are brought from all over the world. They are kept in cages so they can't hurt us or run away. Some animals need to have their cages kept a certain temperature. Alligators and apes are used to really warm weather, so their cages are kept that way. Penguins are used to cold weather and ice, so their cages are cold and have blocks of ice in them.

A lot of the animals at the zoo are from what we call the "cat" family. This includes the lion, tiger, leopard, and cougar. These cats all look different from one another. The leopard has spots, the tiger has stripes, and the lion has a big hairy mane around his face.

At the zoo you will also find several types of bears. The big, white one is a polar bear. The little black and white one is a panda bear, and the biggest bear is called a grizzly.

Activities

1. Find pictures of zoo animals and show them to the child.
2. **10-11-2** Make the wild animal bracelets.
3. **10-11-3** Make a bear puppet. Fold a regular piece of paper (color of your choice) in thirds, much like you would fold a letter. Paste the edge down. Now curve the narrow top edge to form the head as shown in the diagram. Paste the curved edges together. Cut out the other bear parts. Instruct the child to color them and paste the parts to the body.

Discussion (continued)

The biggest animal in the zoo is the elephant. The tallest is the giraffe. Another big, strong animal is the rhinoceros. He has a big horn on the end of his nose.

A favorite kind of animal for children at the zoo are the monkeys. They are so fun to watch. The bigger monkeys are called apes. The biggest monkey is a gorilla. Monkeys like to have visitors and will perform tricks for you.

A seal is also fun to watch. He can clap his fins and dive under the water. He also makes sounds as though he were trying to talk to you.

Activities (continued)

4. **10-11-4** Make a Groovy Gorilla marionette and have him perform for you and your friends.
5. Make a visit to your local zoo and see the animals.

Seasons and Weather
Unit XI

Fall
Lesson 1

Objectives

At the end of the lesson the child will be able to:

1. tell at least one distinguishing characteristic of fall
2. tell what birds and squirrels do in the fall to prepare for winter

Discussion

Fall, or autumn as it is sometimes called, is a beautiful time of year. The nights begin to get cooler. Farmers must harvest their crops before it gets very cold so they won't freeze. Children go back to school in the fall after their summer vacations. Leaves on the trees turn colors of red, orange, and yellow. During fall a ring of fat cells forms in the leaf and cuts off the food and water to the leaf. Without food and water, the green (chlorophyll) disappears. This causes the beautiful colors that have been hiding in the leaf to appear. The fall breezes catch the colored leaves and they glide to the ground.

Activities

1. Take two small pieces of paper the size of a nickel and paper clip them to both the front and back sides of a growing leaf. Leave the papers on for three days. At the end of the three days take the papers off. The green will have disappeared where the papers were placed.

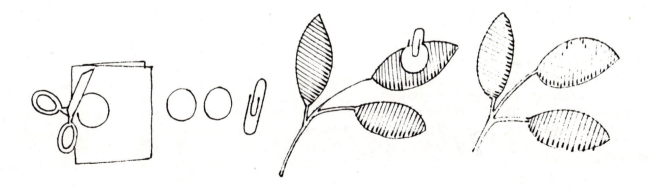

2. Go outside and have the child help you rake leaves, or go to a park and find some leaves that have fallen to the ground. Go for a walk and collect leaves, seeds, weeds, pine cones, etc.

3. Make nature puppets from the things that you have gathered on your walk. Put them together with bits of clay and glue as shown in the diagram. Glue the heads of the puppets on branches. Some children may enjoy just mixing the clay and their nature collections into a collage on a paper plate instead of trying to form a figure.

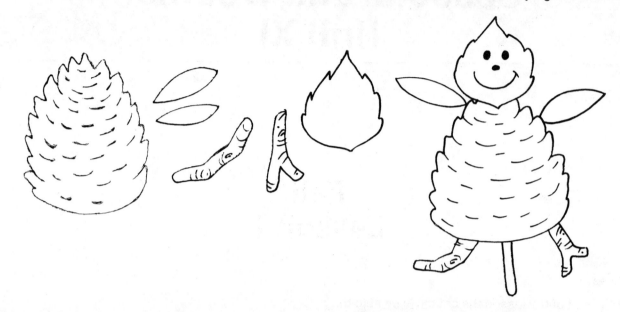

4. Place a leaf on top of a piece of waxed paper. Scatter crayon shavings on top of the leaf. Place another piece of waxed paper on top of the shavings. With a cool iron, press the waxed papers together. The shavings will melt and make the leaf very colorful. Trim the waxed paper to the desired size.

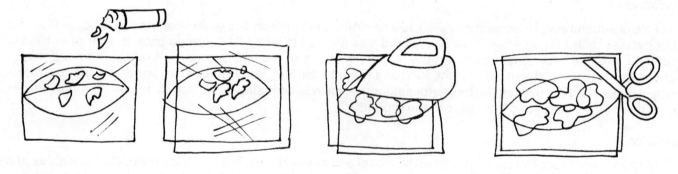

5. Place a piece of plain paper over the top of a leaf. Rub a crayon over the paper, and it will make an etching of the leaf.

Discussion (continued)

In the fall birds and animals prepare for winter. Birds fly south where it will be warmer and they can find food. In cold climates it is nearly impossible for most birds to find seeds, worms, and insects to eat.

Squirrels, chipmunks, and ground hogs all collect nuts, acorns, and fruits during fall. They store them securely hidden away in their homes to eat during the winter. Often a squirrel will store up to a bushel of nuts! He can even store two of the nuts in the pouches of his cheeks.

Activities (continued)

6. **11-1-6** Make a bird with wings that flap.
7. **11-1-7** Make a squirrel. Put two nuts or something a squirrel could eat inside the two pouches.
8. Let the children pretend like they are squirrels. You hide acorns around the room and instruct the children to gather them up to store for the winter.
9. P. E. Suggestion: Creative movement—dance like falling leaves.

Winter Weather
Lesson 2

Objective

At the end of the lesson the child will be able to recognize different types of winter weather such as fog, snow, and hail.

Discussion

In winter we see all types of weather conditions—fog, snow, rain, and hail. Stormy weather causes the sky to turn gray. Fog occurs when the wind blows warm air over a cold surface. This sudden contact with the cold creates moisture in the warm air. Fog looks like grayish-white clouds, feels damp, and is hard to see through.

Activities

1. Experiment with fog. Boil water in a tea kettle. When the steam escapes and hits the cool air, have the child watch it turn into droplets. If it is cold outside, have the child breath on a cold window and see the fog his warm breath makes.
2. Help the child draw a simple picture of an outdoor scene. Color tissue paper gray. Put the tissue paper over the picture and paste or staple it at the top. Have the child lift the tissue paper up and down to signify the fog lifting.
3. Make glass wax. Use recipe found in the recipe section. Let the children draw with it on the windows.

Discussion (continued)

Snow is frozen water that forms into crystals. No two snowflakes are alike. Snow falls in the colder parts of the world and is like a white blanket covering the earth. A lot of our water comes from snow after it melts. Hail is frozen rain. It sometimes can be as big as a golf ball by the time it hits the ground. Hail falls more in warmer climates where snow probably wouldn't fall. Snow makes it very cold outside.

Children play in snow and use it to build things such as snowmen, snowballs, and houses. In fact, some people in really cold climates build their houses out of snow. This kind of house is called an "igloo."

Activities (continued)

4. Make a snowflake out of a white piece of paper as shown. Fold a paper in fourths, draw a snowflake and cut.

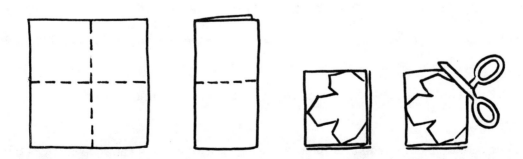

5. Make artificial snow using the recipe found in the recipe section.
6. Make a snow ice cream soda using the recipe found in the recipe section.
7. Make a snowman by taking a white paper lunch sack and stuffing it with newspaper. Staple it shut at the top. Tie crepe paper around the sack about two-thirds up for a bow tie. Make a black hat and staple it on its head.

Make eyes, nose, and mouth. Put buttons down the front. Stick drinking straws in the sides for arms and legs. You can also use thin tree limbs for arms.

8. Let the child be creative and try building an "igloo" with sugar cubes. Use glue or frosting to stick the cubes together.

Winter People and Animals
Lesson 3

Objectives

At the end of the lesson the child will be able to:

1. tell why he should wear warm clothes in winter and be able to name at least three articles of winter clothing
2. tell why ground hogs, bears, etc., sleep in the winter or explain what hybernation is

Discussion

Many animals put on their winter coats. They do this by growing more hair that is thicker and longer. Bears, dogs, and horses are just a few examples of this. We also need to dress more warmly in the winter. With the snow and cooler temperatures, we need to protect ourselves from the weather.

There are many fun winter sports for people to participate in. A few are skiing, ice skating, and sledding.

Activity

1. **11-3-1A, 11-3-1B** Cut out the paper dolls. Dress them in their winter clothes provided.

Discussion (continued)

Many animals cannot find the food they need to survive in winter. These animals such as bears, squirrels, and ground hogs hybernate. This means they find a hole under the ground, a tree stump, or a cave and sleep during the winter months. Since they are sleeping, they don't need to eat—just as you don't need to eat while you are sleeping at night.

The bear sometimes wakes up and checks outside to see if the harsh part of the winter is over. If it is not, he goes back into his cave and hybernates some more.

The ground hog goes to sleep in his winter quarters. He curls himself up in a little ball with his paws under his nose. He keeps them warm by breathing on them. There he sleeps all winter. However, the story goes that he suddenly wakes up on February 2. He stretches himself, rubs his eyes, and creeps out of his hole or nest. If he comes out and it is wet with a gray cloud overhead, he stays out. But if he comes out and sees his shadow, he pops back into his nest as fast as he can and sleeps for another six weeks.

Activity (continued)

2. **11-3-2A, 11-3-2B** Make a ground hog and his house.

Spring Rain
Lesson 4

Objectives

At the end of the lesson the child will be able to:

1. explain where rain comes from and what happens to the rain after it reaches earth
2. identify thunder, lightening, and rainbows

Discussion

In spring we put away our heavy winter coats and clothes and start wearing jackets or sweaters. We can play outside more. Every day is getting warmer and warmer.

In the springtime it rains a lot. What special clothing do we wear in the rain? (raincoat, umbrella, rubber boots, hats)

Activities

1. **11-4-1** Using the paper dolls that you cut out from a previous lesson, put on her spring clothes.

Discussion (continued)

Ask the child where a raindrop falls once it leaves the cloud. Example: on the ground, flowers, pond, house, tree, people, or animals. Even though we cannot see it happen, a lot of the rain that falls goes back into the air when the sun shines on the earth, lakes, and oceans. This is done by a process called evaporation.

When the water in the air becomes heavy, it forms tiny particles of water which come together to form clouds. When the water drops become too heavy and large, the water falls to the earth in the form of rain. The rain comes down in different ways. It can pour, drizzle, shower, or come in a big thunderstorm.

Activities (continued)

2. Demonstrate rain for the child by using a spray bottle filled with water. Spray it and point out to the child where the water falls.
3. Draw a big raindrop for the child; cut it out. Instruct the child to draw and color a picture inside the raindrop of what the rain might fall on when it drops from the clouds.

Discussion (continued)

When it rains we sometimes have thunder and lightening. Lightening is a quick line of light that you see in the sky. Thunder is the loud sound you hear after the lightening strikes.

After a rain storm, we sometimes see a beautiful rainbow. Sunlight is not really just white or yellow. A rainbow is made up of seven different colors. When a ray of sunlight passes through a raindrop, the rain bends the light ray and causes it to break into many colors. (demonstrate with a glass prism)

Rain helps make things grow and gives us water to drink. It also fills our lakes and streams back up after a hot summer.

Activity (continued)

4. Make a rainbow on a white piece of plain paper. The rainbow colors are: violet, indigo, blue, green, yellow, orange, and red. The colors usually blend together so you only see four or five colors clearly. Instruct the child to use at least three of the above colors.

Spring Growing Things
Lesson 5

Objectives

At the end of the lesson the child will be able to:

1. plant his own bulb or seed and watch it grow. From this experience he will be able to tell that all growing things need water, sun, and soil.
2. name one characteristic of the spring season

Discussion

In the spring farmers plant their crops, and people in the city plant flowers and vegetable gardens. The rain helps to water the newly-planted gardens. The wind helps to spread the seeds around, and the sun helps them to grow.

Trees and flowers soon begin to blossom or bud. They later turn into fruit, leaves, and flowers. Sometimes the blossoms look like popcorn hanging from the trees.

You can plant flowers as bulbs, seeds, or startlings. In late spring flowers begin to bloom and make our yards and streets look beautiful.

Activities

1. Fill a paper cup three-fourths full of dirt. Make a face to go on the front of the cup out of construction paper. Paste it on. Plant grass seed in the dirt and watch the grass grow to look like hair. The child can cut the grass when it gets long and pretend he is cutting hair.

2. Make a simple drawing of a tree with many branches. Instruct the child to glue popcorn on the branches for blossoms. Another way to depict blossoms would be to twist short pieces of pink crepe paper and paste them on the branches.

3. Go on a walk and look at the new growths on shrubs, trees, and flowers.

4. Make egg carton flowers as shown below. Cut out each section of the carton where the eggs were placed. Cut petals by shaping each piece according to your preference. Then stick pipe cleaners through the center for a stem.

5. Let the children pick some dandelions. Split their stems up into small strips. Place them in cold water and watch the strips curl up.

Spring Wind
Lesson 6

Objective

At the end of the lesson the child will be able to name at least three ways wind can be a helper. Each child will experience the movement of wind for himself.

Discussion

What is something that you cannot see that is usually outside? You can hear it whistle and feel it on your face. *Answer:* wind.

Activity

1. Put a paper cup or piece of paper on the table and blow it off. Let the child try it. Blow in and out and point out to the child that he can make a little wind himself. Blow other objects of different size and weight such as a feather, cotton ball, piece of cardboard, paper clip, etc. Then compare the difference in movement of the lighter and heavier objects.

Discussion (continued)

The wind is sometimes rough and cold, but it can be our helper. The following are a few of the ways wind helps.

    A. Farmers have big pin wheels called windmills. The wind blows the blades around and makes the mill do certain kinds of work like moving water or grinding grain.

    B. When a bird gets too tired of flapping his wings and flying, he can coast on the wind and it will keep him up.

    C. The wind also helps airplanes fly, gliders stay up, and parachutes float softly to the ground.

    D. The wind and sun help dry our clothes on a clothes line.

    E. The wind blows seeds around so they can grow and replace trees and plants that have died.

Activities (continued)

2. **11-6-2** Make a pinwheel.
3. **11-6-3** Make a wind whistle.
4. Help the child fly a kite in the wind.
5. Let the child blow bubbles. A recipe is included in the recipe section.

Spring Birds and Animals
Lesson 7

Objective

At the end of the lesson each child will be able to tell about one spring activity of a bird and another animal.

Discussion

When the cold winter is over, birds fly back from their winter stay in the south. They search for a good place to build a nest. Usually it will be in a tree, attic, or on the roof of a house. They build their nest to lay eggs and hatch their new babies. There is even a type of bird called the Chimney Swift that builds his nest in a chimney.

Activities

1. Go on a hunt and find things birds could use to build a nest. Examples: scraps of material, yarn, leaves, twigs seeds, etc. Have the child mix them all together and stick them onto clay that has been formed into the shape of a nest.
2. Make a special treat called "Chocolate Nest." A recipe is included in the recipe section.
3. Make a bird feeder. Dip a pine cone into a fairly thick flour and water mixture. Stick seeds onto the pinecone. The flour and water mixture will act as glue. Hang the pine cone on a tree and the birds will eat from it.

Discussion (continued)

Bears, squirrels, and other animals come out of hibernation in the spring. Snakes come out from under rocks. They coil together and shed their skin. Salmon fish go back up the river where they were born and lay their eggs.

Activity (continued)

4. **11-7-4** Cut out the coiled snake.

Discussion (continued)

Since it is getting warmer, many animals shed their hair in spring. It thins out so they won't be too hot in the summer sun. You may have noticed this if you have a dog. This is also the time when we sheer sheep and use their extra fur to make wool.

Activity (continued)

5. **11-7-5** Cut out the lamb. Instruct the child to glue cotton balls or popcorn on the drawing and make believe it is wool. Bits of white yarn could also be used.

Summer
Lesson 8

Objectives

At the end of the lesson each child will be able to:

1. list four summer articles of clothing and tell why he can wear them in summer
2. tell two characteristics of summer and name two summer activities
3. distinguish between hot and cold temperatures by touch and by reading a thermometer

Discussion

In summertime the temperature gets hotter. Children get out of school for summer vacation, and pretty flowers are in full bloom. When it is hot, the temperature on the thermometer reads high; when it is cold, the thermometer reads low.

Activities

1. Place a thermometer in a bowl of cold water. Show the child how low the mercury is. Place the thermometer in a bowl of hot water. Show the child how high the mercury has climbed.
2. Make candy using a candy thermometer. Use the recipe for "Butterscotch Patties." Check the temperature periodically and show the child.

Discussion (continued)

We need different temperatures in our home for different reasons. Where are some cold places in our home? (cold water tap, refridgerator) Where are some hot places ? (furnace, stove, water heater, iron)

Activity (continued)

3. Instruct the child to find a cold place and a hot place or thing in the house. Next have him feel the different temperatures of water that come out of the tap.

Discussion (continued)

The hotter it gets, the lighter we dress. In summer we wear shorts, sandals, sunsuits, and sleeveless shirts. We do different things in hot weather than in cold weather. We can go on picnics, swim, sun bathe, play in the sand, and go on a vacation. You can visit an amusement park, a zoo, lake, mountains, and canyons.

Activities (continued)

4. **11-8-4** Cut out the summer clothes for the paper doll.
5. Go on a picnic lunch today.
6. Make a sand picture. Instruct the child to drip Elmer's glue over a piece of paper in a creative design. Then put sand over the glue. Wait a minute or two and shake off the excess sand.

Discussion (continued)

In the summer we like to eat and drink cold things. It makes our bodies seem cooler. Sometimes if we stay out in the sun too long we will get a sunburn. If we play too hard in the sun, we will get tired and thirsty. That is the time to take a rest and have a cold drink.

The hot summer sun helps the flowers, trees, and shrubs grow. It also helps the farmers crops grow so that we will have plenty of food to eat.

Activities (continued)

7. Make frozen pops using the recipe found in the recipe section.

8. Pick some flowers. They could even be wild ones such as sunflowers or dandelions. Put them in a vase of water.

9. Press one of the flowers by putting it between pages of a heavy book. Put plain paper on either side of the flower to prevent any staining.

10. Dry a flower. Use a box or old cake pan and put sand in the bottom. Place the flower on top of the sand and sprinkle sand in a fine stream over the flower and down onto the petals. Leave the sand on for a week to ten days. Then uncover the flower very carefully and you have a dried, preserved flower. Commercial sand for drying flowers is available in stores, if you prefer.

Holidays
Unit XII

Halloween
Lesson 1

Objectives

At the end of the lesson each child will be able to:

1. tell what "trick or treat" means at Halloween time
2. name two fictional characters associated with Halloween

Discussion

Halloween is celebrated in America on October 31 of each year. This holiday is also celebrated in many other countries. In fact, many of the traditions we have concerning Halloween came from other countries. The Romans honored the Apple Goddess at Halloween. They would play games like bobbing for apples. This is where you fill a container with water and float apples on top. A person tries to get an apple by biting it with his teeth and not using his hands. Sometimes your face gets wet, but it's fun anyway!

Halloween comes in the fall of the year just before wintertime. During this season there are a lot of pumpkins grown in gardens. If you hollow out a pumpkin and carve a face in it, you have a jack-o-lantern. On Halloween night, we put candles in the jack-o-lantern to light up its face. In the olden days, people would light their jack-o-lanterns and it was thought that this would frighten the winter away. They wanted the warmer weather to last longer.

Halloween is a fun holiday for boys and girls because they get to dress up in costumes, carve jack-o-lanterns and go trick-or-treating. Do you know what it means when someone comes to the door and says "trick or treat"? It means that young Halloween visitors will not play a trick on you if you will treat them. When your grandparents were as young as you are, people did not give out as many treats on Halloween as they do today. Children would get all dressed up like demons, ghosts, and witches and play jokes or tricks on people. It's much safer, nicer, and more fun today to get treats. You must remember, though, to only eat those treats that are wrapped up and only go trick-or-treating to homes of people we know or that are in our immediate neighborhood. You should never go trick or treating alone, but should be accompanied by an adult or older child. To help you see and let cars know where you are, you should carry a light with you. When you see other children dressed up like ghosts and goblins, you don't need to be scared because these characters are just make believe, and they won't hurt you.

Activities

Note to Instructor: The following activities should be done over a period of six or seven days prior to Halloween.

1. **Witch** The supplies you will need are:

white or gray cardboard egg carton
black construction paper
yellow yarn

scissors
glue

Cut away four egg slots as a whole piece from an egg carton. The top two egg slots will be the witches eyes. Cover the eyes with black construction paper to cover the holes where the eggs would have been. Cut a black triangular hat as shown and place on the witch's head. Use yellow yarn or crinkled black strips of paper for her hair.

2. **Light bulb witch** the supplies you will need are:

light bulb (can be burned out)   black construction paper
paints   scissors
toilet roll tube   glue
yellow yarn

Cover an empty toilet roll tube with black construction paper. Paint a face on one side of the light bulb as shown Paste a paper cylinder type hat on the light bulb and yellow yarn on each side for hair. Place the light bulb's narrow end down into the toilet roll tube. Add arms or any other features as desired.

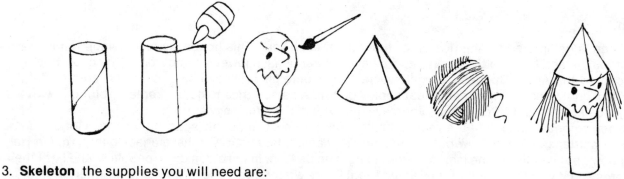

3. **Skeleton** the supplies you will need are:

foam packaging chips   black construction paper
foam from a meat package   glue

Cut a head shaped like a skeleton and paste it on black paper. Paste the peanut-shaped packaging chips on to form arms, body, and legs as shown in the diagram.

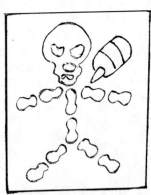

4. **12-1-4** Find the halloween objects in the worksheet picture.
5. **12-1-5** Let the child color and cut out the eyes of the mask. Attach the mask to a popsicle stick so the child can hold it up to cover his face.

6. **Costume Wig** the supplies you will need are:

small lunch sack
scissors
black magic marker

Cut out a hole in front of the sack big enough to expose just the child's face, assuming the child had the sack on his head. Cut strips of the sack to make bangs and hair on the sides. You may want to color the sack black where the cuts will be before cutting. Let the child wear the sack over his head as a wig.

7. **Halloween Brews** see recipe section under Orange Halloween Brew and Rootbeer with dry ice.

8. **Ghost** the supplies you will need are:

assorted round suckers
white Kleenex tissues
narrow white yarn

Wrap the tissue over the sucker; twist and tie a piece of yarn around the neck of the sucker to secure the Kleenex. Dot two black eyes on the face of the Kleenex.

The New World Indians
Lesson 2

Objectives

At the end of the lesson each child will be able to:

1. name two articles of clothing worn by the New World Indians
2. tell what a tribe is

Discussion

A man called Christoper Columbus sailed from England across the ocean and discovered a "New World". He named it America. There were people living on this new land and Columbus named them Indians. They had dark coarse hair, dark eyes, and darker colored skin. Their dress consisted primarily of skins of animals and blankets woven from fibers of plants. The Indians' fancier costumes were heavily ornamented with beads, feathers, and shells. They would also wear earrings, necklaces, and bracelets that add to the splendor of their showy festivities.

Activities

1. Help the child make an Indian jacket. Take a big paper shopping sack that you would get at the supermarket and turn it inside out so the writing will not show. Starting at the open end, cut up the center back of the bag. When you reach the bottom, cut around to make a hole for the head of the child. Then cut across the two side panels of the bag and down about 3 inches to form a sleeve opening on each side as shown. Help the child cut fringe with his scissors along the bottom edge of the jacket, up the front opening, and on the flaps above the arm holes. Instruct the child to color or paint his jacket with a design of his choice.

  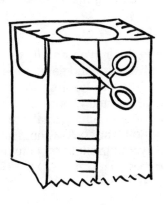

2. Make an Indian necklace. The supplies you will need for this activity are:

straws (colored)	macaroni
paper hole punch	string
colored paper	scissors

Cut the straws into one inch strips. Cut up pieces of colored paper in little shapes and punch a hole through them. You could color the macaroni, if desired. Use the recipe for colored macaroni in the recipe section. Cut a string to the desired length for the necklace and string the straws, papers, and macaroni on alternately. Tie the necklace at the back.

Discussion (continued)

The Indians lived in big groups called tribes. The tribes were really a sort of family united by a common belief or religion. They also had many customs or rituals that were the same.

Each group of Indians had a symbol to represent its tribe or family. This symbol was called a totem. Different objects were carved into the poles such as birds, fish, and animals. Then they were painted with bright colors. Every totem pole was different and when they were completed and put up, the tribe would hold a big feast and celebration.

Each tribe had a leader who was called a chief. The chief would wear a full-feathered headdress. Many other Indians wore headdresses too. They would receive a feather for each courageous deed they performed.

Activities (continued)

3. Make your own totem pole. Take three empty soup cans and cover them with construction paper that the child has drawn objects on. Stack the cans on top of each other. You could also use shoe boxes in the same manner.

4. Make a headdress by cutting a strip of construction paper the length of the child's head. Paste on real colored feathers or feathers made out of construction paper. Have the child think of acts he could do to earn the feathers in his headdress either as a pretend Indian or a helper to his teacher or family.

New World Indians Food and Customs
Lesson 3

Objectives

At the end of the lesson each child will be able to:

1. name one crop grown by the Indians in the New World
2. name one thing the Indians made to help them with their hunting, cooking, or gardening

Discussion

The Indians lived chiefly by hunting and fishing for food. They made their own weapons by hand, out of rocks such as flint and sandstone. They made spears, knives, arrows, and fish hooks.

In addition to hunting for food, the Indians raised crops such as corn, rice, and tobacco. Some Indians even raised pumpkins, squash, and melons.

The Indians had to make all of their own dishes for cooking and eating. These were made out of clay, shells, or hollowed-out stone. The clay dishes were called pottery. The Indian women were the ones who made the pottery and took care of the home. They would also cook and weave and grind the corn so they could make bread from it.

Activities

1. Help the child make a clay pot or bowl using the *clay* recipe in the recipe section.
2. Let the child help you make either Indian Hoe Bread or Indian Fry Bread. Both of these recipes are found in the recipe section.

Discussion (continued)

The Indian women learned to make beautiful baskets by weaving grass and small twigs together. They would use these baskets to carry things in. The women also worked out in the gardens during the day. When they had a small child, they would just strap him to their backs. This was called a papoose. The baby was very content to be with his mother, and she could continue to work.

The male Indians were called braves. They did the hunting and fishing. When their sons were old enough, they would teach them to hunt, fish, and make weapons.

Activities (continued)

3. Show the child something that has been woven such as a mat or a basket. Let him try weaving for himself using strips of construction paper.

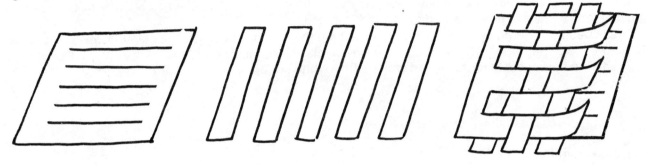

4. **12-3-4** Make an Indian mother and her papoose.
5. Help the child make a papoose to put on his back. Follow the diagram and directions below. You will need:

Poster board   lunch sack
Brown construction paper   string
ric-rac   scissors

lunch sack (body)

ric-rac (headband)

Cut a large sheet of heavy poster board in half and round one of the small ends. Cut a round piece of brown or tan construction paper for the papoose's head. Let the child draw a face on the head. Glue ric-rac across the forehead for a headband. Paste the lunch sack on the poster board below the head for the body. Punch four holes (two at the top, two at the bottom) as shown in the diagram. Thread strings through the holes on each side. Make the strings long enough so the child can put his arms through and wear the papoose on his back.

Thanksgiving
Lesson 4

Objectives

At the end of the lesson each child will be able to:

1. tell why the pilgrims came to America
2. tell what kind of homes the pilgrims built to live in after they arrived in America

Discussion

Several hundred years ago in England people were not allowed to worship as they pleased. The King of England wanted everyone to be a member of his church, the Church of England. A group of men, women, and children didn't want to be members of the King's church, so in order to worship the way they wanted, they had to come to America. It would be a long, hard journey across the ocean for these people. America wasn't like it is today. They didn't know if they could find food and shelter to survive when they arrived. There weren't big cities, towns, or stores where they could just buy what they needed. They had to bring with them what they could and then make and grow the things that they needed.

These people traveled by ship to America. The ship they used was called the "Mayflower" and the people in it were called "pilgrims." These pilgrims wore special clothing. The girls wore black dresses with white aprons and the boys wore black hats, and shirts with a white collar.

Activity

1. **12-4-1A, 12-4-1B** Make the pilgrim hats.

Discussion (continued)

The pilgrims knew very little about America, and they were frightened to come to the new land. They missed the beautiful homeland they were born in, and did not know what America would look like. When they arrived, they were pleasantly surprised to find that America was a beautiful country with great forests, many streams, plants, and animals. They landed at plymouth, Massachusetts and eagerly set about making a new home for themselves.

One of the first things the pilgrims had to do when they arrived was build homes to keep them from the cold weather that would soon be approaching. They cut down trees and made houses out of them. These houses were called log cabins. Everyone helped build each other's houses so they all would be safe before winter came.

The pilgrims also had to plant crops and grow food to help them survive through their first winter. They made friends with the Indians. One Indian named Sequanto showed the pilgrims how to plant corn that would grow. They also caught fish and saved fruit and dried it for the winter months ahead.

Activities (continued)

2. **12-4-2A, 12-4-2B** Find the pilgrim paper dolls and their clothes.
3. See log cabin in Homes Unit, Lesson 1, for additional log cabin activities.

Thanksgiving Day
Lesson 5

Objectives

At the end of the lesson each child will be able to:

1. tell why we celebrate Thanksgiving Day in America
2. name two foods traditionally eaten at Thanksgiving time

Discussion

The first winter spent in Plymouth was very hard on the pilgrims. Nearly half of the colonists died because of sickness, cold, or lack of proper food. New hope grew in the colony, though, after that first winter. The corn harvest was good and made the pilgrims very happy. The governor of the colony, William Bradford, decreed that December 13, 1621 was to be set aside as a day of feasting and prayer in thanksgiving for the success they had had with their crops.

The women of the colony spent many days preparing for the feast. They made journey cake, corn meal bread with nuts, and bread dressing. The pilgrim men caught geese, duck, and fish for the women to cook. The Indians celebrated with the colonists, and they brought wild turkey and deer meat to the feast. For dessert, the women made pumpkin stewed in maple sap. It tasted a little like pumpkin pie.

Activity

1. Make pumpkin bread with the children. The recipe is found in the recipe section.

Discussion (continued)

Everyone ate outside at the big tables. They spent three days feasting, praying, and singing. Every year the colonists continued to celebrate after the harvest. Finally, in 1863, President Lincoln issued a proclamation that officially set aside the last Thursday of November "as a day of thanksgiving and praise to our beneficial fathers."

Thanksgiving is a joyous day! It is usually celebrated with big dinners and happy reunions with family members and friends. It is also a time for serious thinking about our many blessings and the things we are thankful for today.

Most Americans today have turkey and dressing, cranberry sauce, and pumpkin pie as part of their Thanksgiving dinner. What do you have at your house?

Activities (continued)

2. Ask each child to think of something he is especially thankful for, such as home, family, eyes, ears, food, etc.
3. Make a triangle turkey our of colored construction paper as shown in the diagram below.

4. Make gum drop turkeys; the children can eat them when they are done or take them home as a special favor. See diagram below.

5. Make a hand turkey as shown below. Help the child trace his hand and then add the head features, legs, and feet.

Christmas
Lesson 6

Objectives

At the end of the lesson each child will be able to:

1. tell why we celebrate Christmas
2. name two decorations or characters we associate with Christmas time

Discussion

To the Christian world, Christmas day is a very special holiday, for it is the day we celebrate the birth of Jesus Christ. The *Bible* tells us the story of how Jesus was born. (Luke, Chapter 2)

An angel appeared to Mary and told her she was going to have a son whom she was to call Jesus, the Son of God. She was very blessed to be chosen the mother of Jesus.

Just before Jesus was to be born, Mary and Joseph, her husband, traveled to Bethlehem. Mary rode on a donkey, and Joseph walked beside her. It was a long journey, and they were very tired when they finally arrived in Bethlehem. There were many people in Bethlehem that had come to pay their taxes, so it was a very busy town. Mary and Joseph looked all over for a place to stay, but the innkeepers all said that their rooms were all full. One innkeeper could see how tired Mary and Joseph were and he offered to let them stay in his stable with the animals.

During the night Jesus was born. Mary wrapped him in swaddling clothes and laid him in a manger. There were in the same country shepherds watching over their sheep. Suddenly an angel of God appeared to them in the sky and the shepherds were frightened. But the angel said to them: "Fear not: for, behold, I bring you good tidings of great joy, which shall be to all people. For unto you is born this day in the city of David a Saviour, which is Christ the Lord." The shepherds wanted to see the baby Jesus, so they hurried to Bethlehem and found Jesus laying in a manger.

A bright star shone over the stable where Jesus lay. Wise men searching for Jesus followed the star until they found Jesus. They rejoiced and worshiped him and gave him gifts of gold, frankincense, and myrrh. Jesus grew up strong and healthy to be the Saviour of the world. He showed us the way to live and treat other people.

Activities

1. **12-6-1** Cut out the stand-up figures of the manger scene. Let the children reinact the night Jesus was born.
2. **12-6-2** Help the child make a manger out of a shoe box.

Discussion (continued)

Christmastime also carries with it some wonderful and exciting traditions such as Santa Claus, a Christmas tree, and lots of candy and goodies. It is a time for giving as well as receiving, and a joyous occasion to get families and friends together.

Activities (continued)

Note to Instructor: The following activities should be spread over several days before Christmas, as there are too many of them to try to do in a day or two.

3. Make Christmas Wreath cookies with the children. The recipe is found in the recipe section.
4. Help the children make their own Christmas wreath. You will need:

   paper plates
   green crepe paper
   scissors
   paste

Cut the center out of a paper plate. Cut short strips of green crepe paper approximately 4″ in length. Let the children twist them to get a sort of bow effect. Paste the bows allover the paper plate.

5. Make salt dough Christmas tree ornaments using the salt dough recipe in the recipe section. You can color the dough and use cookie cutters to form the shapes you want. When they are dry, string a ribbon through the top and hang them on the tree.
6. Make a Styrofoam ornament. You will need:

   styrafoam balls
   toothpicks
   fake snow

Stick toothpicks into a Styrofoam ball, leaving at least half of the toothpick visible. Spray the ball and toothpicks with fake snow. Hang on the tree with a paper clip or pin.

7. More Christmas tree ornaments . . . you will need:

   construction paper: red, green, white, and gold
   narrow ribbon of any color; glitter
   tracing paper; glue; pencil
   scissors, paper punch

Make a pattern for a star, bell, and ball. Put the patterns on construction paper and cut out as many as you desire. At the tip of each ornament, punch a small hole to tie a ribbon into. Put a little glue in the center and edges of the ornaments and sprinkle glitter on the glue. Shake off excess glitter, tie a ribbon through the hole, and hang on the tree.

8. Make lacy thread balls . . . children love these. You will need:

   balloons (small and round)
   thread
   liquid starch

Blow up a balloon. Lay a spool of thread on its side in a small bowl of starch. Wrap the soaked thread around the balloon firmly until it is covered. Then cut the end of the thread and smooth it down. Let the starch dry overnight; then pop the balloon and gently remove it. Hang the balls on the Christmas tree.

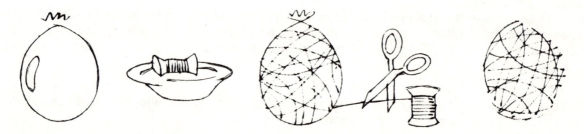

9. **12-6-9** Make a sleigh. You will need:

   sleigh pattern
   red construction paper
   scissors
   glue
   small candy canes

10. **12-6-10** Find the Santa Claus. Color him and then fill his beard in by gluing on cotton balls or crushed egg shells.

11. **12-6-11** Make a Christmas stocking. You can either make it out of paper or felt. Let the children decorate it with glitter, pieces of felt, sequins, etc.

12. Draw a simple Christmas tree on green construction paper for the child. Then let the child paste on fruit loops cereal to decorate the tree. If you use frosting instead of glue, the child can eat his decorations.

Valentine's Day
Lesson 7

Objective

At the end of the lesson each child will be able to express love to someone by giving away a valentine.

Discussion

St. Valentine's Day is celebrated on the 14th day of February in America. At Valentine's Day we think of hearts, lacy doilies, and Cupid with his arrows. At first, people sent gifts with a valentine's verse attached such as "Be my valentine." Today a card with a verse on it is called a valentine.

Valentine's is such a fun day of the year, because we get to let people know we care about them by sending them a valentine. Sometimes it is fun to put a surprise inside the valentine envelope like a heart-shaped sucker or a stick of gum and candy heart.

It used to be that valentines were supposed to be a secret as to who sent them. Today we usually sign our names to the valentines we send, but we can surprise someone by leaving the valentine on their doorstep, ringing the door bell, and then running away before they see us.

Activities

1. Read the child some verses found on valentines. Let the child try making up his own verse.
2. Help the child make a valentine—you will need:

red construction paper	scissors
white paper doilies	ribbon
glue	pens
glitter	

Let the child be creative. You could first cut out a red heart for the child and let him glue the doily in the center. He could decorate around it with bits of paper ribbon, glitter, etc. You may want to write the verse he made up in the center. He can give this valentine to a friend, mother, neighbor, or whomever he chooses.

3. Make a valentine holder—you will need:

red construction paper	glue
white doilies	scissors

Cut out two large hearts from red construction paper. Fold the top edge of one heart down as shown. Cut a doily in half and paste it under the folded edge. Now glue the outside edges of the hearts together. Let the child put his valentines inside the pocket at the top.

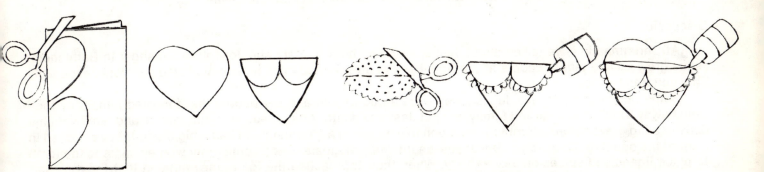

4. Cut out various sizes and colors of hearts from construction paper. Let the child glue the hearts together to make insects, flowers, or animals. They can really use their imagination with these hearts. Here are a few ideas:

5. Doily picture—you will need:

poster paints	doilies
brushes	paper

Have the child place a doily on top of a piece of plain white paper. Instruct the child to paint over the top of the doily. The paint will only fill in where the holes are, and when you take the doily off, the child will have a beautiful design picture.

6. Make frosted, heart-shaped sugar cookies using the recipe in the recipe section for sugar cookies. Let the children help you frost them. Popsicle sticks make good frosting knives for children.

7. Make a valentine tree—you will need:

empty thread spools	red construction paper
pipe cleaners	scissors
foil	glue

Instruct the child to cover each spool with foil. Cut several small hearts out of the red construction paper. Paste them at the top of the pipe cleaners to make flowers. Now push the pipe cleaners down into the spool hole to make a tree.

8. Make a heart-shaped pizza. You will find the recipe in the recipe section—just form the dough into a heart. Let the children help you decorate the pizza with olives, mushrooms, cheese, etc.

Easter
Lesson 8

Objective

At the end of the lesson each child will be able to tell why we celebrate Easter.

Discussion

At Christmastime we talked about Jesus, who was born to Mary and Joseph in a manger in Bethlehem. Jesus grew up and taught people about God. He was a very good man, and Jesus loved everyone, especially little children like you.

Some people did not love Jesus. They were afraid of him and the people that followed him. They took Jesus away from his friends and family and put Jesus to death. After Jesus died, his friends and family put his body in a big grave called a tomb. It was much like a cave in a mountain and had a big stone that was rolled in front of the opening. Three days after Jesus' death, Mary Magdalene and some other women came to the tomb to place linens and spices on Jesus' body. When they approached the tomb, they noticed that the rock had been rolled away. Jesus' body was gone, and they feared some evil people had taken it. An angel appeared to Mary and told her that Jesus had risen from the dead, as He said He would. Jesus had died and become alive again. This is called being resurrected. Jesus died for all of us that we might be resurrected and live again.

We celebrate Easter because that is the day Jesus was resurrected. It comes on no fixed date; Easter is always celebrated on a Sunday in March or April. Easter time comes in spring when the grass is growing, trees are blossoming, and flowers are budding. Everything seems new and fresh in the world. People like to buy and make new Easter outfits, too.

The Easter bunny is said to come on Easter morning and leave a basket of Easter eggs and candy for good little girls and boys.

Activities

1. Easter eggs

A. *Paper collage eggs*-Glue torn or cut tissue paper to blown-out eggs with white glue or liquid starch.

B. *Striped eggs*-paint an egg with white glue and wrap it with rows of colorful yarn. Push the rows together with a toothpick.

C. *Dip and Dye eggs*-stick a pattern of masking tape on a plain egg. Press it securely in place. Dip it in a dark vegetable coloring or Easter egg dye. After it dries, remove the tape. Leave the masked areas white or dip the egg again in a lighter color.

D. *Waxed eggs*-Draw a heavy crayon pattern on an egg. Dip it in a dark color. Melt the crayon marks by putting the egg in a 200° oven for a few minutes. Dip in a lighter color to fill in the pattern you drew with the crayon.

E. *Seed eggs*-Roll eggs first in white glue and then in split peas, poppy seeds, fennel, barley, or sunflower seeds. Kids love to do these.

2. **12-8-2** Instruct the child to complete the figure-ground worksheet. Find the hidden bunnies and eggs.

3. Make an egg mosaic picture. Draw a simple outline of an egg or bunny for each child. Break up egg shells and glue them to fill in the object you have drawn. You may want to color the egg shells.

4. Make an egg bunny—you will need:

hard boiled egg	pen
small paper cup	construction paper
cotton balls	scissors
glue	

Cut small bunny ears out of construction paper and glue them on the small end of the egg. Draw eyes, nose, and whiskers on egg for bunny's face. Cut a hole the width of the bottom of the egg in the bottom of a paper cup. Set the egg in the hole as shown in the diagram. Glue a cotton ball on the side of the cup for a bunny tail.

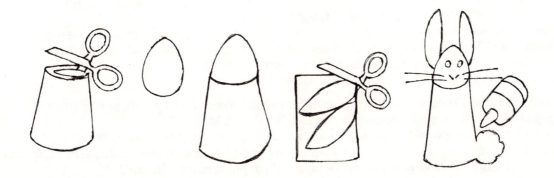

5. Make an Easter Bunny bag—you will need:

medium-sized grocery bag	construction paper
scissors	straws or pipe cleaners
glue	pencil
tape	

Measure down from the top of the sack 9″ on each side and draw a pencil line across the bag. Next, draw two curved lines as shown from the top corners to the first line. Make two large eyes out of construction paper and paste them on the front of the bag. A triangle could be cut for a nose, and the mouth drawn on with a pen. Cut along the ear lines and across the head line through both thicknesses. Tape the ears at the top. Push pipe cleaners or straws through both sides of the nose for whiskers. Fill the basket with fake grass and colored eggs.

6. **12-8-6** Instruct the child to finish the worksheet.

7. If you would like, refer to Animal Unit, Lesson 2, Activity 2, for a bunny hat pattern.

Unit XIII
Music

To The Instructor: Music plays a big part in a preschooler's curriculum, but at this age music should be mostly for his pleasure and enjoyment. Your goal in teaching him about music should not be with the intent of teaching him a skill or expecting a polished performance. He can, however, be taught awareness to contrasts in music such as fast, slow, high, low, loud, and soft. He will be responsive to simple rhythms and body movements associated with the different songs he is taught.

Teaching a song to a preschool child is not difficult. They learn quickly, if you choose simple songs that tend to be repetitious. They love to sing and love to hear you sing. They don't care or won't know if you are "off key", but they will sense your enthusiasm and want to join in. You'll never have a better audience! The following are some simple suggestions for teaching a preschooler a song:

1. Sing the song through several times for the children so the melody and words are clearly heard.
2. If the song tells a story or is for a special occasion, tell the child.
3. If there are any words or phrases that a child might not understand, briefly explain them.
4. Do not teach the words of a song separately from the melody, as it will only confuse the children.
5. Let the children hum the tune with you, filling in words or phrases as they can.
6. If a song is long, you can sing the first part of a phrase and let the children complete the phrase. However, it is better not to break up a song in this way, unless it is long and difficult.
7. Repeat, repeat, and repeat!
8. Use pictures which portray the sequence or the story of a song.
9. Do not try to conduct a song as you would for a congregation of adults. Simply indicate the height and depth of the notes by raising and lowering your hand.
10. Only use accompaniment when the entire song is learned well.

What Music Is and How It First Began
Lesson 1

Objectives

At the end of the lesson each child will be able to:

1. name two things that make music around us
2. tell the difference between a slow and fast rhythm

Discussion

Do you know what music is? It can be almost any sound around us like birds singing, waves splashing upon the shores of rivers and oceans, or the wind as it whistles through the trees. It can be dogs barking or horns honking. Nobody really knows how music first began. Some say it started when cavemen made drums and beat on them. They hollowed out a log, stretched an animal's skin across it, and beat on it with a stick. Some say music started when we sang with our voices. There is music all around us. Today more people can hear and enjoy music than ever before. A phonograph, radio, or television can bring good music into everyone's home.

Have you ever started to tap your feet or shake your head to the beat of the music when you listen to it? Even little babies will bob their heads and kick their feet to music. This beat is called rhythm. There are fast rhythms and slow rhythms. A fast rhythm makes you want to jump up and dance around. A slow rhythm makes you want to relax and be quiet. Have you ever heard a mother sing "Rockabye Baby" to her baby at bedtime? This song has a slow rhythm and helps calm and quiet a baby so he can go to sleep.

Activities

1. Make a drum out of an empty oatmeal or hat box for each child. Let him use a dowel, spoon, or rubber spatula for a drumstick.
2. Play a song with a fast rhythm and let the children creatively dance to it.
3. Play or help the children sing Rockabye Baby to their dollies, as if they were trying to get their dolly to go to sleep. They may rock it in their arms or pretend to rock it in a cradle.
4. Teach the children one or two of the songs in the music section and make one of the rhythm instruments suggested on the following pages.

How Music Is Made
Lesson 2

Objectives

At the end of the lesson each child will be able to:

1. tell what a note is and distinguish whether it is high or low by sound
2. name at least two musical instruments

Discussion

Have you ever wondered what makes all of those beautiful sounds that are in a song you hear on the radio or a record player? Our voices make music when we sing, and there are usually musical instruments that play along with a singer. Can you name any musical instruments that you have seen or might have in your own home? (piano, guitar, drum, horn, flute, etc.) These instruments play sounds called notes. These notes are written down to make a piece of music that tells the musican which notes to play when. There are high notes that can sound like a siren or whistle and low notes that might sound like a grizzly bear or perhaps your Daddy's voice, and there are notes in between. When these different-sounding notes are put together, they make a melody or song.

When several instruments are played together, they are called a band or orchestra. Have you ever seen marching bands in parades? They are all carrying their instruments with them and playing as they march along. When several people sing together, they are called a chorus or choir. Have you ever sung Christmas carols with many friends or family members? You were part of a chorus, if you sang with them.

The person who leads a song for a chorus or orchestra is called the conductor. Without him, people wouldn't know when to begin and stop or when to play loud or soft. He leads with his arms and usually holds a baton in one of his hands. A baton is a long, narrow stick that he waves back and forth to the beat of the music.

People have been writing songs for many, many years. Songs can make us feel happy when we are sad. Do you have a favorite song you sing that makes you happy inside? Certain songs remind us of holidays and special occasions. What does the song "Jingle Bells" remind you of? It's fun to get together with others and dance and sing to music. Maybe one day you will sing in a choir or play in a great orchestra. Can you think of an instrument you would like to learn to play?

Activities

1. **13-2-1** Find the notes and staff. Let the children paste the notes on the staff any way they want, as if they were making up a song.
2. Let each child make a band instrument from the suggestions on the following pages. Let each child take a turn playing conductor and leading the band.
3. Visit a band practice at a school near you. Teachers are usually very cooperative and even let the children walk around and touch the different instruments.
4. **13-2-4** Teach the children one or two of the songs in the music section. For this lesson, teach "If You Chance to Meet a Frown" and tell the children they can sing this when they get sad to make them happy again. An interchangeable face is included as a visual aid.
5. Fill pop bottles with different amounts of water and let the children blow across the top to make different tones.
6. **13-2-6** Help the child complete the worksheet on musical instruments.

Easy-to-Make Musical Instruments For Children

Body Rhythm Instruments

whistling   click tongue
humming   speak—ha, ha; ho,ho
hissing   slap thigh
snap fingers   sh-sh-sh
stomp feet

Rhythm sticks

Use dowels or spoons; strike together on top of an aluminum pie plate or bowl.

Drums

Use an empty oatmeal or hat box or large metal cans. Strike with a dowel, spoon, or rubber spatula for drumstick.

Hummers

Save cardboard tubes from the inside of toilet paper rolls. On one end of the tube, punch a hole, using a paper punch and punching down as far as possible on the tube. Cover that same end of the tube with either waxed paper or aluminum foil. Secure this covering with an elastic, but make sure that the punched hole is not covered. Tell the children to put their mouths up to the open ends of the tubes to blow and hum at the same time.

Cymbals

Use kettle and pan lids with knobs and sound them together.

Plucking Instruments

Make a rubber-band banjo by obtaining a sturdy open box. Stretch a few rubber bands of different sizes, spaced widely, around it.

Bells

1. string bells on a strong string and tie the ends
2. sew bells onto a mitten
3. sew bells across the top of a wide elastic band
4. drill holes in bottle caps, string them on a string, and tie the ends together.

Washboard

Paste corrugated cardboard onto heavy cardboard or plywood. Let the child strum it with a spoon, dowel, or nail.

Shakers

Fill empty containers with dried beans, macaroni, paper slips, small rocks, popcorn, or rice. You could use bandaid boxes, baby food jars, small milk cartons, jello boxes, etc.

Tambourine

Pin small bells around a sturdy paper plate and shake.

Pipe-sounding Instruments

Fill five or six sturdy real-glass glasses with water, each at a different level. Let the children make musical tones by tapping against the glasses with a metal spoon. Different amounts of water make different pitched tones.

Fill pop bottles with different amounts of water and blow across the top of them to make different pitched tones. The bottles could also be tapped.

Sandpaper blocks

Saw two 5″ lengths of 2″ x 4″ wood. Cut two pieces of 00 sandpaper 4″ x 5″. Paste the sandpaper to the blocks of wood and let dry. Rub the blocks together to the beat of the music.

Songs for Preschoolers

I'm A Little Teapot

I'm a lit-tle tea-pot short and stout Here is my han-dle here is my spout.

Put hands behind back and sway side to side.

Put left hand on hip when singing "handle."

When I am read-y then I'll shout Tip me o-ver and pour me out!

Put right hand up and out when singing "spout."

Tip to right side on "tip me over."

Playmate Song

Row, Row, Row Your Boat

Row, row   row   your   boat   gent - ly   down   the   stream,

Have children sit down on floor and pretend to row.

Mer - ri - ly, mer - ri - ly,   mer - ri - ly, mer - ri - ly   life   is   but   a   dream.

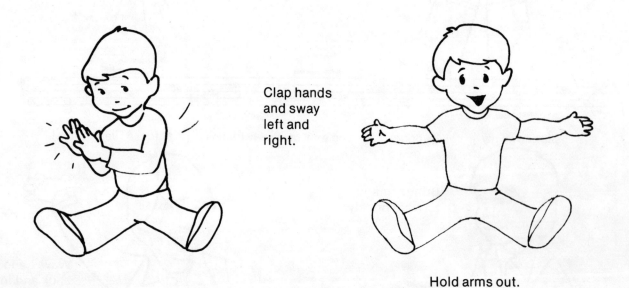

Clap hands and sway left and right.

Hold arms out.

Hickory, Dickory Dock

Hick - o - ry dick - o - ry dock. The mouse ran up the clock. The

Sway arm
down and
up again
like a
pendulum.

Move arms up
and wiggle fingers.

clock struck one, the mouse ran down, Hick - o - ry dick - o - ry dock.

Clap
above head.

Move arms down
and wiggle fingers.

Sway arm
down and up
Again like
a pendulum.

If You're Happy and You Know It

Other actions for additional verses: stomp your feet; shake your head; touch your nose; jump up and down; click your heels, etc.

The Farmer In The Dell

Note: Children form a circle with one child inside acting as the "farmer". They join hands, sing, and march around the farmer until he chooses a wife, etc. The cheese begins again as the farmer.

Other verses:

The farmer takes a wife, etc.   The dog takes a cat, etc.
The wife takes a child, etc.   The cat takes a rat, etc.
The child takes a nurse, etc.   The rat takes a cheese, etc.
The nurse takes a dog, etc.   The cheese stands alone, etc.

Mary Had a Little Lamb

Other verses:

And everywhere that Mary went,
Mary went, Mary went,
Everywhere that Mary went,
The lamb was sure to go.

It followed her to school one day,
School one day, school one day,
Followed her to school one day,
Which was against the rule.

It made the children laugh and play,
Laugh and play, laugh and play,
Made the children laugh and play,
To see a lamb at school.

Old MacDonald Had A Farm

Other verses:

ducks; quack, etc.
turkeys; gobble, etc.
pigs; oink, etc.

cows; moo, etc.
donkeys; he, haw, etc.

Children can take turns holding pictures of animals, and it will help the children keep the song in sequence.
Farm animals are pictured in Activities 10-10-1A, 10-10-1B, and 10-10-1C.

Jack and Jill

Jack and Jill went up the hill to get a pail of wa-ter.

Raise hands up and pretend to walk up hill.

Hold arms to form pail of water.

Jack fell down and broke his crown and Jill came tum-bling af-ter.

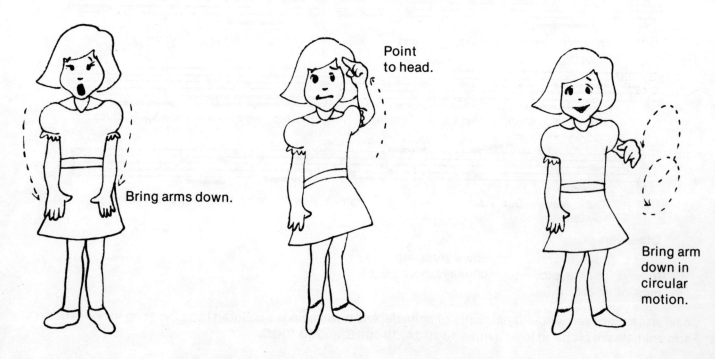

Bring arms down.

Point to head.

Bring arm down in circular motion.

Oats, Peas, Beans, and Barley Grow

Oats, peas, beans, and bar - ley grows, Oats, peas, beans, and bar - ley grows, Nor

you nor I nor an - y one knows, How oats, peas, beans, and bar - ley grows.

Point to
neighbor on "you."

Point to
self on "I."

Hold arms out
on "anyone" and
shake head
back and forth.

Other verses:

Thus the farmer sows his seed,
Stands erect and takes his ease,
He stamps his foot and claps his hands,
And turns around to view his lands.

Waiting for a partner,
Waiting for a partner,
Open the ring and take her in,
While we all gaily dance and sing.

Now you're married you must obey,
You must be true to all you say
You must be kind, you must be good,
And make your husband chop the wood!

The remaining verses can be acted out by the children according to the words.

London Bridge

Lon - don Bridge is fall - ing down, fall - ing down, fall - ing down,

Lon - don Bridge is fall - ing down, My fair la - dy.

Note: Let two children represent the bridge by joining hands and raising them to form an arch. The rest of the children, in single file, pass under the bridge. When the words "My fair lady" are sung, the two children forming the bridge let their arms fall and catch whichever child is passing under.

Other verses:

Build it up with iron bars, etc.

Iron bars will bend and break, etc.

Build it up with pins and needles, etc.

Pins and needles rust and bend, etc.

Build it up with penny loaves, etc.

Penny loaves will tumble down, etc.

Build it up with gold and silver, etc.

Gold and silver I've not got, etc.

Here's a prisoner I have got, etc.

What's the prisoner done to you, etc.

Stole my watch and broke my chain, etc.

What'll you take to set him free, etc.

One hundred pounds we have not got, etc.

Then off to prison he must go, etc.

Take the key and lock him up, etc.

Rockabye, Baby

Note: Let child pretend he has a baby and he is trying to rock it to sleep while he sings this song.

Twinkle, Twinkle, Little Star

If You Chance To Meet A Frown

Second verse:
No one likes a frowning face
Change it for a smile.
Make the world a better place
By smiling all the while.

Note: Let the children take turns holding the frowning face and changing it to a smile. It is included in the book.

Unit XIV
Physical Education

Non-locomotive Skills—exercises or skills that are done in one area without moving from place to place; non-locomotive movement lends itself to creative movement.

1. **Bend and Stretch** (these movements can be done in several positions, standing, lying)

   a. bend your back forward; now bend your legs; stretch out straight
   b. play follow the leader—bending and stretching different ways
   c. call out different parts of the body to bend
   d. stretch like you are just getting up
   e. stretch tall and bend small
   f. bend pretending you are an elevator going up and down
   g. bend one arm and straighten the other
   h. see how much space on the floor you can take by stretching out in all directions.

2. **Twist and Turn**

   a. stand against the wall; turn at waist and touch hands on wall; return to the front and turn to the other side.
   b. twist different body parts—neck, waist, etc.
   c. dance the "twist" to some fast music
   d. make ¼, ½, and ¾ turns facing different directions
   e. twist your head to see as far back as you can

3. **Swing and Sway**

   a. sway back and forth like a tree does in a breeze
   b. swing your arms around in opposite directions
   c. swing a pretend bat or golf club
   d. swing your legs back and forth while holding onto a wall or chair.
   e. sway your head back and forth
   f. swing your arms like you are swimming; try to back stroke
   g. make circles with your arms, changing the size of the circles

4. **Rise and Fall**

   a. get up from different levels—back, sitting, kneeling
   b. fall from different levels—sitting, kneeling, standing
   c. pretend you are a plant and grow
   d. play cowboys and fall when you get shot
   e. pretend you are a snowman melting away
   f. slowly float down like a leaf in autumn

5. **Push and Pull**—pushing is moving a force away from the body; pulling is moving a force toward the body.

   a. Tape a line on the floor with masking tape and do the following activities with a partner:

      1. grasp hands and try to pull partner over line
      2. get behind your partner and try to push him over the line
      3. have a tug-of-war with a rope and try to pull the other side over the line

Locomotive Skills—exercises or skills where you move from place to place. Examples: walk, hop, jump, skip, run.

1. **Walking** —stress to the children that they should have good posture and point feet forward while walking.

   a. walk forward and backwards, left, right, and diagonally.
   b. walk sideways
   c. walk high on your tip toes and then low
   e. walk softly and then noisily
   f. walk using giant steps and walk using small steps
   g. move or do other skills with arms or head while walking
   h. walk quickly and then slowly.
   i. mark a space on the floor and have children walk inside it without touching anyone. Keep making the area smaller and smaller (could use any shape)
   j. have a walking race
   k. walk and then freeze on a signal given by the teacher; you could use music and stop it at different intervals
   l. walk forward for 8 counts and then change direction
   m. walk with your partner facing you; go backwards and forwards
   n. walk in various directions and clap hands alternately with the beat of the music
   o. walk on heels and then on toes
   p. put some music on slow speed and walk in slow motion
   q. imitate the way certain animals walk—elephant, cat, etc.
   r. lift legs high and march
   s. make stilts for a child to walk on; you will need:

   two 46-ounce cans   nail
   hammer   string

Punch a hole on each side of the two cans as close to one end of the can as possible. Put string or rope through the holes, leaving enough to tie around a child's foot.

2. **Running**

   a. run and stop on signal—could use music or a whistle, etc.
   b. run low and get higher until you are on tip toes.
   c. run and change directions on command
   d. run with large steps and then with small ones
   e. run in place
   f. run like a tortoise, then like a hare
   g. run as fast as you can, then as slowly as you can
   h. play this game with a partner: one person runs and tries to dodge the other who must stay within one yard of the person running. On signal, both stop and trade positions
   i. lift the knees as high as possible while running
   j. run and touch different spots on the wall or floor
   k. have a running race
   l. run within a designated area and do not touch anyone
   m. play "Red light Green light" one person is at one end of the room facing the wall. The other children are at the other end of the room facing the person at the end of the room. The person alone calls out green light and all of the other children run to touch him before he calls out red light and turns around. The first child to touch the "green light" person is the winner

3. **Leaping**—a movement in space with a transfer of weight from one foot to the other. It is an extended run done more easily if combined with running.

   a. have child see how far he can leap
   b. have child see how far he can leap straight up into air
   c. have child run three steps and then leap three times in a row
   d. hold hands with a partner and leap; then run three steps and leap again
   e. run and leap to music on a certain beat or word in the song
   f. leap over an object
   g. leap and reach as high as you can
   h. play leap frog; one child leaps while another crouches down

4. **Jumping**—take off from both feet and land on both feet.

   a. jump high
   b. take little jumps
   c. land noisily—than land softly
   d. jump in several directions—forward, backwards, and sideways
   e. see how far you can jump; have a contest with the other children
   f. jump like a kangaroo
   g. jump with your legs and arms stiff, like on a pogo stick
   h. jump and turn in the air
   i. jump slowly and then jump fast
   j. cross feet and jump

   ### Jumping Games

   a. **Jump the Brook**—Make a brook by putting two strips of scotch tape down on the floor, placed so they get increasingly farther apart to form an arrow. Instruct the child to start jumping at the narrowest part, spreading his legs as he jumps outside the lines. See how far he can go without touching the lines. Make sure he lands with bended knees.
   b. **Hide and Jump**—Have the children form a circle. One player is "it" and leaves the room while the children choose someone to hide a small paper under his foot. "It" comes in, stands in the center of the circle, and calls jump. All children in the circle jump up. "It" tries to quickly look around the circle and find who is hiding the paper under his foot, then he guesses who it is. If he is right, he gets to keep being "it"; if he is wrong, the person who hid the paper gets to be "it".
   c. Instruct one half of the children to scatter all over the floor and get in a crouched position. The other half of the children jump over the crouched children on signal. Then both groups change positions.

5. **Hopping**—transfer of weight from one foot to another foot

   a. hop on one leg and then change legs
   b. see how high you can hop
   c. see how far you can hop
   d. hop on a line; do small hops and then large hops; cross back and forth over the line
   e. draw a circle and hop in and out of it
   f. do different things with arms and legs while hopping
   g. hop and turn around
   h. hop forward, backwards, and in different directions
   i. trace out objects while hopping
   j. round your back and arms and hop like a bouncing ball

6. **Skipping**—a series of step-hops done with alternate feet. To teach a child to skip, ask him to take a step with one foot and then take a small hop on the same foot. Then do the same thing with the other foot—step, then hop. Skipping is hard for a preschool child to do, so just keep practicing throughout the year.

   a. skip to music
   b. hold hands with a partner and skip

   After the child has mastered all the locomotive skills, combine the skills and do different activities.

   1. follow the leader—use locomotive skills
   2. to music, start one locomotive skill and then switch at command
   3. have races or relays doing one skill down and another back, or do simple combinations
   4. beat a drum to various rhythms and call out different skills to do to the rhythms
   5. have children close their eyes and do different locomotive skills

   ### Stunts and Tumbling

1. **Balancing**

   a. balance an object on your hand (plate, small book, bean bag)
   b. balance a light book or paper plate on your head; try walking
   c. make a small obstacle course and have the child go through it while balancing an object on his hand or head
   d. try taking a small jump, hopping, skipping, or runing while balancing a small object on hand or head

e. do the kangaroo hop—hold arms close to sides with elbows bent up and palms facing down; put a bean bag or other object between the knees and move in different directions, taking small jumps

2. **Balance Beam**—use a chalk line, tape, or rope

   a. have child walk across a narrow width and try to stay on it
   b. try walking tippy-toed on a line
   c. follow steps; the front foot moves forward and the back foot moves up; one foot always leads
   d. heel-toe—take regular steps, each step put the heel next to the toe
   e. hop on a line
   f. balance—touch. An object (eraser, block, paper) is placed a foot away from a line. Balancing on one foot, the child touches the object, and recovers to the starting position.

3. **Body Balance**

   a. balance on one leg and then do the following:
      1. put hands on head, fold across chest
      2. roll up on foot without falling
      3. bring knee up on other leg; close eyes and see how long you can balance
   b. balance on knees, kneel down, point feet to rear, lift feet off the ground and balance on knees
   c. lame dog—put your weight on hands and knees; bend one leg off the floor and crawl forward
   d. balance on your front; lay down on stomach and:
      1. lift up head
      2. lift up arms and head; put arms forward and backward
      3. lift one leg, then the other; lift both legs at the same time
      4. lift both legs and arms and head
   e. cross-legged stand—stand with legs crossed and:
      1. do a windmill by touching opposite hand to opposite leg
      2. bend up and down with arms out front and then on hips
      3. try to walk, then increase speed
      4. try to sit down with legs crossed; then try to stand up

4. **Creative Movement with Balance**

   a. pretend you are a circus performer:
      1. a seal balancing a ball on his nose
      2. a tight-rope walker
      3. a big elephant lifting up leg, 2, then 3 legs

Rolling

1. Side Roll—lie on back; bend the knees to chest with arms crossed, hands on shoulder; roll to either side
2. Roll over by dropping the shoulder and tucking both the elbow and knee under; roll over completely on the shoulders and hips, coming to hands and new position
3. On back, wrap arms around bended legs and rock from side to side
4. Head—touch: Have arms outstretched backwards for balance; lean forward slowly and touch head
5. Forward Roll—kneel on the mat, put hands on mat in front of knees; put head on mat between hands; tuck in chin on chest; a push off with the hands and feet provides the force for roll:
   a. have child squat in roll
   b. do several forward rolls in succession
   c. roll over an object
6. Log Roll—lay on stomach and roll over and over again
7. Back roll—start in crouched position with toes and knees together and hands resting on the floor; roll backwards and then forwards; try to keep a rhythmic backward, forward motion.

Stunts

1. **Bear Walk**—bend forward with hands and feet on the ground; have arms and legs straight; travel forward by moving the hand and foot of the same side together; then move the other side.
2. **Elephant Walk**—bend forward; clasp hands together to make a trunk; walk forward, keeping legs straight and swinging the trunk.

3. **Seal Walk**—lay on stomach; support body with weight or hands and legs extended behind; walk forward on hands and drag feet.
4. **Rabbit Jump**—stoop to the floor with knees apart; arms are between the knees with the hands placed on the floor ahead of the feet. Move forward by reaching out first with both hands and then bring both feet up to hands. If can also be done with arms on outside and legs on inside.
5. **Bouncer**—one person (the ball) squats and holds the knees with the arms. The partner (bouncer) stands behind with his hands on the "ball's" upper back. The bouncer pushes the ball and makes it bounce.
6. **Top spin**—stand with the feet apart; jump, turn, and land facing one-quarter turn to the right; jump, turn, and land facing one-half turn to the right, etc. Repeat the entire sequence to the left.
7. **Heel Click**—stand with the feet about 12 inches apart. Jump into the air and click the heels together and land with the feet apart.
8. **See-Saw**—partners face each other and join hands; one partner stands and the other squats. Partners move at the same time and each finishes in the opposite position. Repeat at a faster rate of speed.

Manipulative Activities

1. **Bean bags**—Bean bags, paper or foil balls, yarn balls, or pom poms are good to use for a child's first throwing and catching experience. Using a softer object helps build confidence in catching and throwing. There are several simple ways to make a bean bag. Take an old sock and cut off the bottom foot area; sew and then fill it. You can also cut off the toe part, fill and tie both ends, and you have a bean bag. A very simple throwing object would be to tightly fold together a pair of socks. A yarn ball is also very good, and you can make a pom-pom out of yarn. Follow the diagram below:

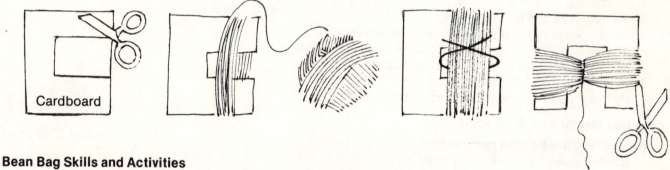

Bean Bag Skills and Activities

  a. throw a bean bag to a partner using an underhand toss
  b. throw the bean bag in the air and catch it; toss it with one hand, then the other, then both hands; toss using the back of the hand
  c. toss and catch from different levels, sitting, kneeling, and standing
  d. toss the bean bag in the air, clap and then catch it
  e. throw a bean bag at a target; make the clown; cut out and paste it on a box and throw bean bags through its mouth
  f. toss a bean bag into the waste basket
  g. from different levels—stand on a chair, sitting, etc., hit the clown's, or a waste paper basket's, mouth
  h. throw a bean bag as far as possible and go pick it up
  i. toss a bean bag to yourself, using different parts of the body—elbow, foot, instep, head
  j. balance a bean bag on different parts of the body and try to move around
  k. make a scoop and toss the bean bag and catch it in the scoop. Use an empty Clorox bottle as shown:

Games with Bean Bags

1. **Birds on a fence**—get a board or balance beam and put bean bags across it. Try to hit the bean bags or birds off the fence.
2. **Kitten in a Basket**—let each child have his turn tossing bean bags into the empty basket. Each time a child gets a bean bag in the basket it counts as a kitten; the child with the most kittens in the basket is the winner.
3. **One Step**—Throw the bean bag to a partner; after each catch, move back one step and see how far you and partner can throw and still catch the bean bag.
4. **Toss to the Leader**—Make a line; the leader throws to each person in line; if someone drops the bag, he goes to the end of the line. If the leader drops the bag, he goes to the end of the line and the person at the front becomes the leader.
5. **Bean Bag Horseshoe**—a mark is put on the floor; the bean bag closest to the mark gets a point; if the thrower gets right on the mark, he gets two points.
6. **Cat and Mouse**—One bean bag is called the mouse and is passed around the circle. The other bean bag is called the cat and is passed around the circle in the same direction. When the cat reaches the mouse, the game is over. (use different colored bags)

Ball Rolling Skills

1. While sitting roll ball to partner.
2. While sitting roll ball against the wall.
3. Stand up and roll the ball forward; run and stop it or catch it.
4. Have a partner stand apart and roll ball between his legs.
5. Put scotch tape down in a straight line on the floor; roll the ball along the line.
6. Roll the ball into a tipped-over box.
7. Roll the ball backwards through legs.
8. See how far you can roll the ball.
9. Roll the ball to a partner standing up with legs apart. Make sure it rolls on the floor; don't throw it.
10. Set up blocks or plastic bottles; roll a ball and knock them down.
11. Have the child lie on the floor with a ball under his stomach and roll around, manipulating himself with his arms and legs.
12. Fold a blanket in a rectangle. Have a person at each end; roll a ball in the blanket back and forth trying to keep it from falling off the blanket.
13. Make an obstacle course and roll the ball through or between things such as chairs, pillows, and tables.
14. Sit on the floor with legs open and roll a ball back and forth between each other's legs.
15. Play "Break the Circle". One child is "it". He stands in the middle of the circle. The other children form a circle standing in the stride position with their feet touching. "It" tries to roll the ball between their legs and out of the circle. If a person in the circle stops the ball before it goes out, he gets to be "it".

Ball Bouncing Skills (use soft balls)

1. Have the child use both hands and bounce and catch the ball.
2. Bounce the ball two or three times and then catch it.
3. Sit on the floor and softly bounce a ball.
4. Bounce a ball to a partner.
5. Bounce a ball; clap hands, then catch it.
6. Bounce a ball to music.
7. Bounce a ball within a boundary.
8. See how many times you can bounce a ball in a row.
9. Use a scoop—throw the ball up and let it bounce; catch it with the scoop.
10. Bounce balls back and forth between partners using scoops.

Manners Game

Instruct the children to stand in a circle with one person designated as "it" who stands in the center. "It" bounces the ball to each person in the circle, and they bounce it back. When they receive the ball they must say "thank-you"; when "it" gets the ball back he must say "you're welcome". If anyone forgets, the person who said the magic words last is now "it".

Catching the Ball

1. Catching with arms—Hold arms in front of body partially bent; the fingers are spread and curved. The arms and hands look like a basket; catch the ball in the basket.
2. Catch with hands—keep hands cupped and catch the ball.

Activities

1. Throw the ball up and catch it in your arms.
2. Catch a ball in your arms tossed by a partner.
3. Let a ball bounce once and then catch it.
4. Catch a tennis ball in your hands—have partner throw it.
5. Bounce a tennis ball against a wall and catch it with both hands.

Game: Children all stand in a circle. One child is "it" and throws the ball up in the air and calls out another child's name. That child must catch the ball while it is in the circle.

Physical Activity Games

1. **Hot and Cold**—Decide on a task in your mind for a person to do such as sweep the floor, stand on head, play piano, turn on lights, etc. When a person gets nearer to the object or task, say you are getting "warmer"; when he has found the object or done the task say "you are on fire!"
2. **Doggie, Doggie, Who's Got the Bone**—"It" sits on a chair blindfolded or with eyes closed with a bone under "its" chair. Someone is chosen to steal the bone. When the stealer is back to his seat, he barks. "It" opens his eyes and tries to guess who has the bone.
3. **Blind Man's Bluff**—One child is blindfolded and is turned around and around in the circle. Take the blind man to an object or person; let him feel it and try to guess what it is.
4. **Spin the Platter**—Spin the platter or plate and catch it before it stops spinning.
5. **Pick up Sticks**—Gather together a bunch of sticks. These could be straws, toothpicks, or matches. Sit around the table or the floor. Give each player two sticks to use in picking up the other ones. Drop a large number of sticks into a high loose pile in the center of the table. Let each child take turns trying to remove as many sticks as possible without making the pile move. When the pile moves, the next person takes his turn, etc., until all of the sticks are picked up. The player with the most sticks wins.
6. **Ring and Pin**—Give each person a dowel or unsharpened pencil. Tie together with a string several canning jar rings or curtain rings for each person. Let the children toss the ring with one hand and try to catch it on their sticks.
7. **Toss Game**—Let the children toss canning jar rings, buttons, pennies, or a rolled pair of socks into different containers such as a box, egg carton, muffin tin, or waste basket. Even a child who is sick in bed can play a toss game. Attach a five foot length of string firmly around a pair of rolled socks and pin the free end of the string to the pillow. Then the tosser can retrieve the ball by pulling on the string.
8. **Farm**—Instruct all the children to form a circle leaving one child in the middle. The child in the middle is the farmer and moves around the inside of the circle calling out names of animals. The circle children imitate the sounds of the animals. The leader calls out, *"Follow me!"* All of the children march around behind the farmer acting like the animals. The teacher may want to be the farmer the first few times until the children get the idea of the game.
9. **Duck Duck Goose**—Have each child sit down and form a circle with one child standing outside of the circle. He touches one child and says "Duck," touches another child and says "Duck," touches a third child and says "Goose." The goose chases "It" around the circle to the "Goose's" position in the circle. If "It" is tagged, he is "It" again. If "It" gets to the place, he stays there and the other player becomes "It."
10. **Objects Go Around**—Have all of the children sit down and form a circle. Get three or four different shaped objects and a record player or piano. Distribute the objects around the circle. Start the music and have the children pass the objects around the circle in the same direction. The object is to not be holding an object when the music stops.
11. **Mother, May I?**—This game needs to be played in a large room or gym. Establish a starting and finishing line in the room. One child is "It" and stands near the finish line. The rest of the children stand on the starting line. The object of the game is to reach the finish line first. "It" tells one of the children how many steps he can take and what kind. The steps could vary such as baby steps, scissor steps, giant

steps, or hopping steps. The player must ask, "Mother, may I?" and await the answer before he moves. If he does not ask the question, he must go back to the starting line. Even if the question is asked, "It" may say, "no."

12. **Red Light, Green Light**—Have the children form a single line with one child about twenty feet in front of them with his back to the group. The leader starts by saying "Green Light." The rest of the children may advance toward the end line. When the leader says "Red Light," the children must all stop. The leader then turns around, and if any child is moving after he has said "Red Light," that child goes back to the starting line. The teacher could be the leader for this game.

13. **Kneeling Tag**—Designate a person to be "It." Establish a finish line for the children to run to. "It" chases the other children who are safe if they kneel before "It" gets to them. First one to the finish line without being caught is the winner.

14. **Frozen Tag**—same as kneeling tag, only when tagged they freeze in place. First one frozen is "it" next time.

15. **Doggie, Doggie**—children join hands in a circle. One child stands outside the circle holding a handkerchief. He starts walking around the circle saying, "I have a little doggie and he won't bite you, and he won't bite you, etc. he drops the handkerchief at the feet of a child and says "but he will bite you." The child picks up the handkerchief, chases the child who drops it, around the circle till they reach the same point. The child with the handkerchief now takes his turn.

Creative Movements

Using Action Words or Pictures

1. Find some pictures that have people doing things in them such as riding a horse, running, playing baseball etc. Show them to the children and let them act out what they see.
2. Find objects in pictures such as a train, airplane, elephant, bear, etc. Show these to the child and let him act out what that object might do.
3. Tell the children to make the shape with their body that is shown on a particular card you hold up.
4. Tell the children a story. Everytime you use a certain word, have them do a particular action.

Drama Activities

1. Let the children act out a familiar story or nursery rhyme such as the Three Bears; Three Little Pigs; etc. One fun one to do is Jack Be Nimble; have the children jump over a make-believe candle stick.
2. Let the children act out things they might do such as play in the leaves, fly a kite, ride a bike, or make a snowman.
3. Let the children do simple pantomines and see if the other children can guess what they are doing. Examples: washing dishes, riding a bike, fishing, brushing teeth, etc.
4. Let the children imitate stages of development in a person; crawl like a baby, act like you're first starting to learn to walk, walk like an old grandma or grandpa might walk.
5. Pretend to dance like a ballerina or skate like an ice skater.
6. Pretend to be a soldier, sailor, fireman putting out a fire, etc.
7. Make believe you are a witch—stir the witch's brew, ride a broom, laugh like a witch.
8. Be a make believe person or character such as a dragon, fairy, goblin, ghost, Donald Duck, etc.
9. Pretend to be a particular insect. Be a bee on a flower and then go into the hive and make honey, or sting someone; be a caterpillar and spin a cocoon and come out and flap your wings; be a spider or an ant, etc.
10. Pretend to be different animals such as chick, elephant, rabbit, lion, horse, frog, etc.
11. Let the children pretend to be Superman, Batman, or Wonderwoman. Sew them a cape out of crepe paper, butcher paper, or material. Use a piece of material 12″ × 18″ and sew ribbon around the neck. Make sure the children understand they can't really leap tall buildings!
12. Pretend to be popcorn popping. Curl up in a ball and then pop out with legs and arms spread wide.

Using Objects

1. Hit a balloon around the room to music.
2. Dance around using scarves.
3. Make pom-poms and shake them. Act like you are a cheerleader.
4. Put feathers on strips of crepe paper and let the children run around and dance with them.
5. Use a rhythm instrument and dance or march to your own beat or rhythm.

Recipes
Unit XV

American Cornstarch Pudding

½ cup sugar
3 Tbsp. Cornstarch
¼ tsp. salt

2 cups milk
1½ tsp. vanilla

Mix sugar, cornstarch, and salt in a saucepan. Gradually add the milk and bring to a boil; boil one minute, take off heat, and stir in vanilla. Serves 4. You can add one to two Tbsp. cocoa to make chocolate pudding.

Bubbles

3 cups soap flakes
4 Tbsp. cooking oil

1 tsp. sugar
food coloring

Mix above ingredients together and strain through a cloth; blow through a blower. A concentrated liquid detergent will also work in place of this recipe.

Bunnies on the Lawn

Make one package of lime jello using the directions on the package. Chill the jello in a large cake pan. Place drained pear halves on top, rounded sides up. Use sliced almonds for the bunny's ears and whipped cream for the tail. Raisins or small chocolate chips would be good for the eyes.

Butterscotch Patties

1 cup granulated sugar
1 cup white corn syrup

1 tsp. vinegar
½ cup butter

Put syrup and sugar into saucepan and heat until sugar dissolves. Then add vinegar. Continue boiling without stirring until it reaches 260⁰ F. (hard ball stage) Add butter and continue cooking to 270⁰ F. (soft ball stage). Remove from heat. Drop half-teaspoonfuls of the candy onto well buttered pans to form patties. Let cool before removing from pans. Makes about 40 patties.

Caramel Corn

6-8 qts. popped popcorn
1 cup white karo syrup
1 cube margarine

1 dash salt
1 tsp. vanilla
1 can sweetened condensed
milk

Bring syrup and sugar to a boil. (soft ball stage) Add margarine and sweetened condensed milk, stirring constantly, slowly enough that the mixture does not stop boiling. Bring to medium ball stage; remove from heat and stir in salt and vanilla. Cover the popped corn.

Cinnamon Pinwheels

1 slice white bread
2 Tbsp. milk
½ tsp. imitation butter flavoring

1 tsp. margarine
1 tsp. granulated sugar
½ tsp. cinnamon

Flatten bread with rolling pin. Combine milk, butter flavoring, and brush ½ of mixture on bread. Combine sugar and cinnamon. Sprinkle on bread. Starting at long side, roll bread tightly, cut into 8 slices. Bake at 350° for five minutes. After baking, brush pinwheels with remaining mixture. Makes 8 small pinwheels.

Cheese Fondue

1 large velveeta cheese brick
1 can chedder cheese soup

Melt the cheese in double boiler or microwave oven. Add the soup without diluting. Mix and warm. Dip chunks of french bread in and eat.

Chocolate Chip Cookies (extra large size)

1⅓ cup shortening
1½ cup sugar
1½ cup brown sugar
4 beaten eggs
4 cups sifted flour

2 tsp. baking soda
2 tsp. vanilla
1 tsp. salt
6 oz. chocolate chips or M&N's

Cream together shortening, sugar, and brown sugar. Add beaten eggs. Sift together and add the sifted flour, baking soda, salt, and vanilla. Stir in the chocolate chips and bake 10 minutes at 375°. Make the dough the size of golf balls. Place only six cookies per cookie sheet. Makes 27.

Chocolate Easter Egg Nests

Nest:
1 package (12 oz.) semi-sweet chocolate morsels
2 Tbsp. shortening
cupcake baking cups
⅓ cup sugar
jelly beans

¼ tsp. peppermint flavoring
1/8 tsp. salt
3 drops green food coloring
1 cup heavy cream, whipped
coconut

Filling:
1 package unflavored gelatin
½ cup cold water
1 cup hot milk

Melt chocolate chips and shortening. Pour into baking cups, covering bottom and sides to desired thickness. Refrigerate. Dissolve gelatin in cold water. Let sit for five minutes. In another bowl, mix hot milk, sugar, peppermint flavoring, salt, and green coloring. Stir in dissolved gelatin. Allow to cool, then fold in whipped cream. Add to chocolate formed cups and top with coconut and jelly beans. To serve, carefully remove paper baking cups. Yield: 12 nests

Chocolate Foundue

3½ blocks Hershey's Baking   1 Tbsp. milk
   Chocolate   1½ tsp. vanilla
1 can sweetened condensed   1 Tbsp. creamy peanut butter
   milk   (optional)
½ cup marshmallow creme

Combine baking chocolate and condensed milk in saucepan; stir constantly over medium-low heat until choco-late is melted and mixture is smooth. Blend in marshmallow creme and milk. Just before serving, stir in vanilla and peanut butter. Serve by dipping any fruits into warm fondue: apples, pears, peaches, bananas, strawberries, pineapple chunks, etc.

Chocolate Turtles

2 squares unsweetened   ¼ cup sugar
   chocolate   1 cup flour
½ cup butter or margarine   1 tsp. vanilla
2 eggs

Melt chocolate and butter over double boiler. Set aside to cool. Beat eggs. Mix in sugar. Stir in chocolate mix-ture. Fold in flour and vanilla. Heat waffle iron to medium-low. Drop by teaspoonfuls onto waffle iron. Close lid. Bake 1½ to 2 minutes. Cool. Spread with chocolate frosting. Yield: 3 dozen

Corn Flake Wreathes

Melt in large saucepan 30-34 large marshmallows and stir until blended. Add one tsp. vanilla flavoring or almond extract. Add a small amount of green food coloring. Stir in 4½ cups corn flakes. Drop onto waxed paper by tablespoons and shape into small wreathes. Add cinnamon candies to look like berries. Grease hands before shaping.

Doughnuts (Buttons and Bows)

2 cups bisquick   ½ cup sugar
2 Tbsp. sugar   ⅓ cup light cream
¼ tsp. nutmeg   1 egg
1 tsp. cinnamon   ¼ cup butter or margarine, melted

Heat oven to 400°. Stir bisquick, 2 Tbsp. sugar, nutmeg, cinnamon, cream, and egg to a soft dough. Gently smooth dough into a ball on floured cloth-covered board. Knead five times. Roll dough ½ inch thick. Cut with floured doughnut cutter or improvise. To make bows, hold opposite sides of each ring and twist to form figure "8". Place buttons (holes) and bows on ungreased baking sheet. Bake 8-10 minutes. Immediately dip each But-ton and Bow in melted butter, then in ½ cup sugar, coating all sides. Makes 8.

Doughnuts (especially for preschoolers)

1 pkg refrigerated biscuits   1 tsp. cinnamon
1 cup sugar   vegetable oil

Mix sugar and cinnamon. Set aside. Push a finger through each biscuit to make a very large hole in the center. Heat 1″ deep vegetable oil to 375° in a frying pan. Drop in doughnuts. Cook to a golden brown. Roll in sugar mixture. Yield: 8.

Egg Paint

Beat one egg and add ¼ tsp. water and 1 tsp. karo syrup; add food coloring of your choice. Paint cookies with this mixture.

Finger Jello

4 packages unflavored gelatin ½ cup sugar
1 cup cold water 4 cups boiling water
3 packages any flavor jello

Put ingredients in a 9"x 13" pan in the order given. Stir until well dissolved. Refrigerate several hours or over-night, then cut into 1" cubes. Yield: 12 dozen cubes. Cookie cutters can also be used to cut jello into different shapes. Just let jello set up on a cookie sheet before cutting.

Fingerpaint

2 cups boiling water 2¼ cups soap flakes
1½ cups liquid starch food coloring

Combine boiling water and starch in a bowl. Add soup flakes. Mix thoroughly. Add food coloring of your choice. Refrigerate to cool before using. To store and to keep fresh, cover and refrigerate. Yield: 1 qt.

Cornstarch Fingerpaint

2 cups water
¼ cup cornstarch
Food coloring

Bring water to a boil. Add small amount of water to cornstarch and blend together to make a paste. Gradually add paste to boiled water, stirring well. Bring to a boil. Remove from heat. Add food coloring of your choice. Cool; mixture will thicken as it cools. Yield: 2 cups

Salt and Flour Fingerpaint

1 cup flour ¼ cup hot water
1½ cups salt Food coloring

Sift flour and salt. Stir into hot water. Add food coloring your choice. Yield: 2 cups **Note:** Other finger painting ideas are to use shaving cream or pudding.

Frozen Yogurt Bananas

1 cup unflavored yogurt 5 medium-sized firm bananas
¼ cup honey 1 cup flaked coconut or
  chopped almonds

In a small bowl, blend together the yogurt and the honey. Peel bananas; cut in half crosswise and insert a flat wooden stick into cut end of each half. Dip banana halves in yogurt mixture to coat completely and place them, slightly apart, on a baking sheet lined with waxed paper. Cover with plastic wrap and freeze for about 1 hour. Meanwhile, spread coconut or almonds on an ungreased baking sheet and bake at 350°, stirring often, for about 10 minutes. Cool. When the coating on the bananas is firm, dip each banana in the yogurt mixture again, then roll in coconut or almonds. Return to baking sheet, cover, and freeze. Makes 10.

Frozen Bananas

Peel bananas; roll in melted sweet chocolate. Fasten on popsicle sticks and freeze.

Fudgesicles

1 package chocolate ½ cup heavy cream
  pudding mix 2 cups milk
½ cup sugar

Combine and mix until dissolved. Pour into containers and freeze.

Glass Wax Fun

1 bottle glass wax (find with cleaning supplies in grocery store)

Rub glass wax all over a window and allow to dry. Let child draw on wax with fingers, creating any design. When the child is through, wipe window with a clean cloth.

Graham Crackers Goodies

Boil a can of sweetened condensed milk *in the can* for four hours. Make sure water is covering the entire can. Open the can and spread the contents on graham crackers. Stack the crackers together to make about 10 layers of the frosted graham crackers. Refrigerate overnight and then slice through the layers to cut dessert-sized pieces. Can be topped with whipped cream.

Halloween Brew

2 cups Tang	1⅓ cups sugar
1 package (3 oz.) imitation	1 tsp. cinnamon
lemonade mix	½ tsp. ground cloves

Combine all ingredients together and store in an air-tight container. Add 2 to 3 teaspoons of mixture to 1 cup water for one serving. Yield: 25 servings.

Halloween Witches' Brew

Prepare a bottle of rootbeer extract according to directions. Instead of bottling and adding the yeast, add 2-3 pounds dry ice. It will bubble and excite the kids and they will love the taste!

Hand Cream

12 oz. glycerin	½ tsp. borax powder
1½ cups stearic acid	2 cups distilled water
¼ bar paraffin wax	1 Tbsp perfume
1 Tbsp. ammonia	Few drops food coloring

In a stainless steel or glass double boiler, heat glycerin, stearic acid and paraffin wax. Add ammonia. Beat with electric mixer until milky and until crystals dissolve. Remove from heat. Set aside. Combine borax powder and distilled water. Stir into beaten mixture. Add perfume and food coloring. Beat again until creamy. Yield: 1½ qts. The children should not mix this, but merely watch the teacher. When it is made, they can put the cream into baby food jars to take home.

Hot-Dog-On-A-Stick

1 cup pastery flour or (⅔ cup	⅔ cup milk
cake flour and ⅓ c. flour)	1 egg, beaten
2 tsp. baking powder	12 franks
1 tsp. dry mustard	12 lollipop sticks
¼ tsp. salt	

Mix flour, baking powder, dry mustard, and salt. Sift into a bowl. Stir in milk and egg. Mix well. Insert 1 lollipop stick in the end of each frank and dip into fritter batter. French fry in 360° fat for one minute or until crispy hot. Yield: 12 servings.

Ice Cream (vanilla)

2 cups milk	¼ tsp. salt
1 cup sugar	4 cups light cream
4 Tbsp. vanilla	

Scald milk; add sugar and salt to milk and stir till dissolved. Add cream; stir in vanilla; cool; freeze in ice cream freezer or ice cube trays, or bread loaf pans. Strawberry jam or grated chocolate chips could be added for other flavors.

Ice Cream Cone Cupcakes

1 box cake mix	2 eggs
1⅓ cups water	24 ice cream cones (flat bottomed)

Beat cake mix, water, and eggs with electric mixer for three minutes. Fill cones about ¾ full. Bake at 350⁰ for 30 minutes. Cool and frost. Yield: 2 dozen

Fluffy White Frosting

(makes cupcakes look like ice cream)

1 cup sugar	dash of salt
⅓ cup water	2 egg whites
¼ tsp. cream of tarter	

Combine sugar, water, tarter, and salt in saucepan. Bring to boiling and stir until sugar is dissolved. Very slowly add syrup to two unbeaten egg whites, beating constantly with electric mixer till stiff peaks form—about 7 minutes. Dip cup cakes into frosting, twirl, and pull out to form a peaked top.

Indian Hoe Cake

1 cup corn meal	1 tsp. salt
¼ cup boiling water	2-3 Tbsp. butter or margarine

Place buttered, edged cookie sheet and spatula in refrigerator for 15 minutes. Mix all ingredients in bowl, then rapidly pour onto cookie sheet, spreading evenly. Mark horizontal and perpendicular lines with spatula. Bake at 300° for 45 minutes. Store in air-tight container. Reheat before serving. Yield: 3-4 dozen pieces of cornbread.

Indian Fry Bread

6 cups flour
2 tsp. baking powder
1 tsp. salt

Mix the above ingredients and add enough water to make a soft but not sticky dough. Shape into round, flat patties and fry in oil until brown.

Initial Dough

¾ cup margarine	2½ cups flour
1 cup sugar	2 tsp. soda
1 egg	½ tsp. salt
¼ cup molasses	1 tsp. cinnamon
1 tsp. ginger	

Mix first four ingredients. Sift together the remaining ingredients; mix the two mixtures till smooth. Chill for four hours (optional). Roll into snakes and form letters of the alphabet or the child's initials.

Lemonade

Mix one part lemon juice to five parts water and sweeten to taste.

Lemon Cooler

1 lemon, whole
1 five inch candy stick, raspberry or lemon flavored

Soften lemon by rolling and squeezing in your hands. Cut a hole for the candy stick near the stem part of the lemon. Insert candy stick in lemon and suck as if a straw. The juice flows more freely after awhile.

Colored Macaroni

2 cups straight macaroni
¼ cup vinegar
food coloring

Put the above ingredients in a glass jar with a lid. Shake. When well colored, spread the macaroni out on a paper towel to dry. This takes about an hour, but best if done so it can dry overnight.

Oatmeal Cookies

1 cup shortening	2 cups rolled oats
1 cup granulated sugar	1 tsp. baking powder
1 cup firmly packed	½ tsp salt
brown sugar	1 tsp. cinnamon
2 eggs	½ tsp. clove
1 tsp. vanilla	½ tsp. ginger
2 cups flour	1 tsp. soda

Mix shortening and sugars; add eggs and vanilla. Sift together all the dry ingredients, except the rolled oats. Mix them with the sugar mixture and blend well. Stir in rolled oats. Drop by heaping tablespoonsful on greased cookie sheet. Bake at 350° for 12-15 minutes.

Ooblick (kids love the feel of this)

½ cup water
1 cup cornstarch

Add water and a little bit of cornstarch at a time to form a slimy, semi-runny mixture. Form it into a ball in your hand and then open your hand and let it run through your fingers; repeat. To keep fresh, store in an air-tight container in the fridge.

Orange Julius

1 6 oz. can orange juice	1 cup water
12 ice cubes	3 Tbsp. sugar
1 cup milk	2 tsp. vanilla

Mix the above ingredients in a blender until foamy.

Orange Rolls

2 pkgs. refrigerator bisquits	¾ cup sugar
1 sq. butter or margarine	1 tsp. orange rind

Place last three ingredients in a 9″ x13″ pan in oven to melt. Mix and place biscuits on top of mixture. Bake at 350° for 15-20 minutes.

Paste (cooked)

In a two-quart saucepan mix:

1 cup flour
1 tsp. salt
2 cups water

Add the water slowly, stirring until cooked. Simmer five minutes. Cool and refrigerate in an airtight container.

Paste (thinned white glue)

Mix: ½ cup white glue (Elmer's)
        ½ cup water

Peach Cobbler

¼ cup butter or margarine
1 cup bisquick
½ cup milk
1 cup sugar

⅔ cup sugar
3 peaches
½ cup water

Melt butter in an 8″ × 8″ pan in a hot oven. Mix bisquick, milk, and ⅔ cup sugar. Cook peaches in water and 1 cup sugar. (Can use canned peaches in syrup.) Spoon bisquick over hot butter. Then spoon peaches over bisquick, reserving liquid. Next pour liquid over entire contents. Bake until brown about 20-25 minutes at 350° F. Serves 6.

Peanut Butter Cookies

½ cup butter or shortening
½ cup peanut butter
½ cup sugar
½ cup brown sugar
1 egg

½ tsp. vanilla
1 cup flour
½ tsp. salt
½ tsp. baking soda

Cream together shortening, peanut butter, and sugars. Add egg and vanilla. Sift together flour, baking soda, and salt. Add to mixture and blend well. Form into small balls and place on a cookie sheet. Press the ball flat with the back of a fork. Bake at 350° for 10 min.

Peanut Smoothie

2 cups milk
4 ice cubes
½ tsp. cinnamon

⅓ cup peanut butter
1 Tbsp. molasses

Blend in a blender and serve.

Preschool Pizza

1 package refrigerated biscuits
1 6 oz. can tomato sauce
4 oz. Mozarella cheese, grated

1 Tbsp. oregano or
   Italian seasoning

Separate and flatten biscuits. Spread each with 1 tbsp. tomato sauce. Sprinkle with oregano. Top with 2 tbsp. cheese. Bake at 425° for 12-15 minutes. English muffins could also be used instead of biscuits.

Pizza Dough

1 cup warm water
1 pkg. (1 Tbsp.) yeast
4 cups flour

1 tsp. salt
3 Tbsp. salad oil

In large bowl, dissolve yeast in one cup warm water. Add salt, flour, and oil and mix well. Knead till well blended. Add additional drops of water, if needed. Oil the outside of the dough and place in large oiled bowl to raise. When doubled in bulk, punch down and spread out on cookie sheet or pizza pan. Cover with pizza sauce. Top with cheese, mushrooms, green peppers, sausage, hamburger, or pepperoni.

Peanut Butter Playdough (edible)

1 cup peanut butter
1 cup karo syrup

1 cup nonfat dry milk
¼ cup sifted powdered sugar

Blend peanut butter and syrup in large mixing bowl. Sift dry milk and powdered sugar together and add all at once. Mix all together with a spoon; then with hands, knead in dry ingredients. Use as you would any playdough and the kids can eat it, if they have washed their hands!

Ornament Dough—great for Christmas tree ornaments

4 cups flour
1½ cups water
1 cup salt

Mix ingredients. If clay is too stiff, stir in more water. Dough should be smooth and easy to handle. When thoroughly mixed, remove from bowl and knead five minutes. Shape as desired. Bake at 350° for 45 minutes. Paint, if desired, with magic markers or poster paints.

Playdough (cooked)

food coloring
2 cups water
2 cups flour
1 cup salt

½ cup cornstarch
2 Tbsp. vegetable oil
1 Tbsp. powdered Alum

Add food coloring of your choice to water. Mix all ingredients. Cook over medium heat until thick. Remove from pan and knead until smooth. Keep in refrigerator in airtight container.

Playdough (uncooked)

4 cups flour
2 cups salt
water—enough to make a soft, workable dough

Add water slowly to the flour and salt, stopping when the dough is still a little dry, and begin to work by hand. Knead 10 minutes.

Popsicles

1 package (3 oz.) any
   flavored gelatin
1 cup sugar
2 cups cold water

1 package similar flavored
   powdered punch mix
2 cups hot water

Combine first four ingredients until dissolved. Add cold water and blend well. Pour into containers and freeze.

Pumpkin Bread

5 cups flour
4 tsp. baking soda
1 tsp. salt
1 Tbsp. cinnamon
1 tsp. cloves, ground
1 tsp. nutmeg

4 cups sugar
4 cups pumpkin
1 cup vegetable oil
½ to 1 cup chopped nuts
1 cup raisins
10-14 empty soup cans

Mix flour, baking soda, salt, cinnamon, cloves, and nutmeg. Sift and set aside. Blend sugar, pumpkin and vegetable oil. Gradually stir in flour mixture. Fold in nuts and raisins. Grease cans and fill ½ to ¾ full. Bake at 350° for 1 hour. Let bread cool 15 minutes and then remove from the cans.

Snow (artificial)

2 cups Ivory flakes
1 cup hot water

Put flakes in a bowl and pour hot water over them. Beat with electric mixer until mixture reaches the consistency of thickly whipped cream. To decorate a Christmas Tree, dip hands into "snow" and rub lightly over branches in opposite direction of needle growth. To frost cardboard, use a pastry tube or cookie press filled with "snow".

Snow Ice Cream Soda

1 scoop vanilla ice cream
½ cup milk
1 tsp. honey, warm

1 drop food coloring
fresh-fallen snow

Mix vanilla ice cream, milk, honey, and food coloring in a blender. Put in a tall glass. Fill the rest of glass with snow.

Stained Glass Windows

1 egg
1 cup powdered sugar
1 6 oz. pkg. chocolate chips
1 cup chopped nuts

2 Tbsp. margarine
1 pkg. small colored marshmallows

Beat egg and powdered sugar. Melt chocolate chips and margarine. Add to the egg mixture. Add marshmallows and nuts. Form into 3 long rolls or logs. Roll in graham cracker crumbs. Chill and slice.

Sugar Cookies

1 cup shortening
1½ cups sugar
2 tsp. baking powder

½ tsp. salt
2 eggs, beaten

Cream sugar and shortening. Add dry ingredients, then eggs and vanilla. Add enough milk to make a soft dough. Roll ¼″ thick. Cut out; bake at 350° for 12 minutes.

Surprise Rolls

1 pkg. refrigerated crescent
   dinner rolls
¼ cup sugar
1 tsp. cinnamon

8 marshmallows
¼ cup margarine, melted
8 cupcake liners

Mix sugar and cinnamon. Set aside. Dip each marshmallow in margarine, then in sugar mixture. Separate rolls. Place one marshmallow in center of each triangle. Wrap the triangle points around the marshmallows until it is completely sealed tightly. Pinch all edges. Place in cupcake pan (use liners). Bake at 375° for 10-12 minutes.

Sweetened Condensed Milk

1 cup hot water
2 cups sugar

½ cube butter
4 cups powdered milk
(*not* instant)

Mix all ingredients and use in any recipe that calls for sweetened condensed milk.

Vegetable Dips

Mix one package dry onion soup mix with 1 pt. sour cream or mix one package Uncle Dan's dressing mix with 1 pt. sour cream.